Echoes of Hope

The True Story Behind the Film 'Sound of Hope: The Story of Possum Trot'

Harold M. Alva

Copyright

© 2024 [Harold M. Alva]

All rights reserved. No part of this book may be reproduced, distributed, or transmitted in any form or by any means, including photocopying, recording, or other electronic or mechanical methods, without the prior written permission of the publisher, except in the case of brief quotations embodied in critical reviews and certain other noncommercial uses permitted by copyright law.

Table of Contents

INTRODUCTION 1

CHAPTER 1 11

   THE ORIGINS OF POSSUM TROT 11

      Historical Context of Possum Trot 11

CHAPTER 2 22

   THE STRUGGLE AND RESILIENCE OF THE COMMUNITY 22

      Challenges Faced by the Possum Trot Community 22

      Economic Hardships 23

      Educational Barriers 24

      Social Services and Health 25

      Environmental Challenges 26

      Inspirational Stories of Resilience and Hope 27

CHAPTER 3 36

   THE CALL TO ACTION 36

      The Pivotal Moments 36

      Reverend Martin's Introduction 38

The Initiatives of Susan Ramsey...................................40

The Ripple Effect of Community Action.................41

Building Partnerships and Alliances.........................43

Overcoming Obstacles and Honoring Achievements
....45

CHAPTER 4..50

CONCEPTUALIZING THE STORY........................50

Joshua and Rebekah Weigel's Vision for the Film ..50

Writing the Screenplay..52

Keeping Fiction and Facts in Check..........................57

Challenges and Triumphs...60

CHAPTER 5..63

CASTING AND CHARACTER DEVELOPMENT 63

Selection of Actors...63

A Comprehensive Look into Actor Preparation and
Character Portrayals..68

Collaborative Character Development......................75

CHAPTER 6..79

FILMING IN MACON, GEORGIA............................79

    Choice of Location and Its Significance 79

    Behind the Scenes of the Production 81

    Challenges in Logistics 83

    Memorable Moments 86

CHAPTER 7 94

    BUDGET AND PRODUCTION LOGISTICS..........94

    Managing an $8.5 Million Budget................................94

    Key Production Roles and Their Contributions....101

CHAPTER 8 109

    DIRECTING THE VISION 109

    Joshua Weigel's Directorial Approach 109

    Collaborations 111

CHAPTER 9 121

    EDITING AND POST-PRODUCTION...................121

    Post-production Process: Editing, Sound Design, and Special Effects 121

Balancing Artistic Vision with Technical Execution 127

CHAPTER 10 131

SECURING DISTRIBUTION 131

The Deal with Angel Studios 131

The Marketing Strategies 134

The Film's Title Changed 139

CHAPTER 11 143

ADVANCED SCREENINGS AND INITIAL REACTIONS 143

The Location and Ambience 144

The Screening Experience 145

Initial Reactions from the Audience 147

Important Preliminary Reviews 148

Early Reactions' Impact 151

CHAPTER 12 154

THEATRICAL RELEASE ON JULY 4, 2024 154

Nationwide Release Strategy 154

  Box Office Performance 159

CHAPTER 13 170

 CRITICAL AND PUBLIC RECEPTION 170

  Comprehensive Reviews from Critics 170

  Public Reception and Impact on Viewers 176

  Conversations in the Community and Their Social Impact 177

CHAPTER 14 186

 THE IMPACT OF SOUND OF HOPE 186

  Reflection on the Film's Cultural and Social Impact 186

  The Future of Storytelling Inspired by Real-Life Events 192

CHAPTER 15 200

 CONTINUING THE LEGACY 200

  Ongoing Initiatives Inspired by the Film 200

  How the Story of the Possum Trot Still Encourages Hope and Change 205

  The Broader Cultural Impact 211

Conclusion 213
APPENDICES 215

INTRODUCTION

Foreword by Letitia Wright

Upon initially being contacted by "Sound of Hope: The Story of Possum Trot," I was impressed by the book's remarkable humanism. I have always been drawn to stories that ask us to view the world with empathy and compassion as an actress and activist. That is exactly what this movie is: a ray of optimism, resiliency, and the strength of community. In addition to managing the film's production, my duties as executive producer included promoting the film's message and making sure that viewers could relate to its sincerity.

It was immediately apparent that "Sound of Hope" was a movement rather than just a movie. The tale of Possum Trot, a small, close-knit community enduring great hardship, is proof of the human spirit's unwavering resilience. It is about regular people, motivated by love, faith, and a common dream of a better future, accomplishing incredible things. This story exactly reflects my ideals and the causes I champion, which makes my participation extremely fulfilling and personally personal.

Facilitating the cooperation between the filmmakers and the Possum Trot community was one of my main duties. We had to tell their tale accurately and with the respect it deserved. This required spending time getting to know the inhabitants, hearing about their stories, and appreciating their successes and setbacks. I was able to personally observe the tenacity and fortitude that characterize Possum Trot through these encounters, and I felt this essence needed to be faithfully portrayed on screen.

I collaborated closely with Joshua and Rebekah Weigel, the screenwriters, as we set out on this adventure to make sure the script was accurate to the actual events it was based on and captivating as well. We dug deep into the characters' lives, examining their aspirations, concerns, and motives. This degree of specificity was necessary to craft a story that would appeal to readers and respect the Possum Trot community's past.

"Sound of Hope" is significant in ways that go beyond its story. It acts as a reminder of the strength of the human spirit and the advantages of group effort. This movie emphasizes the beauty of togetherness and the strength that comes from sticking together in the face of difficulty in a society where differences frequently cause division. It is a call to action, imploring us to stand by one another and have faith in the potential for good change, despite how overwhelming the circumstances may appear.

I was involved in the distribution and marketing plans as an executive producer. To guarantee that the movie was seen by as many people as possible, the strategic choice was to collaborate with Angel Studios, a business renowned for its dedication to powerful narrative. The triumph of "Sound of Freedom" showcased the studio's capacity to captivate audiences with significant content, and our goal was to emulate this achievement with "Sound of Hope." It was intentional to release the movie on July 4, 2024, a day that represents freedom and unification, to emphasize its message.

"Sound of Hope: The Story of Possum Trot" is a celebration of the human spirit rather than merely a movie. It's about trusting in the strength of community and optimism and finding light in the darkest of circumstances. I feel a sense of pride and thankfulness as we tell this tale to the globe. Being a part of this production has been an honor, and I can't wait for viewers to see Possum Trot's amazing journey. I hope it encourages you to view the world with optimism and work toward a brighter future for everybody, just as it has encouraged me.

Introduction

The events that inspired "Sound of Hope: The Story of Possum Trot" are true stories that capture the spirit of community, hope, and resiliency. The process of creating this movie was just as amazing as the tale it portrays, full of obstacles, victories, and inspiring moments. This introduction seeks to give a synopsis of the occasions that served as the film's inspiration as well as the creative process that brought it to life.

Possum Trot is a sleepy little town that has seen a lot of hardship. Its citizens showed an amazing capacity for love and support despite the difficulties. Our film is based on a true story about Susan Ramsey and Reverend Martin, who, along with their community, set out to improve the lives of individuals with whom they came in contact. Despite all the obstacles in their way, their narrative is one of unyielding faith and a dogged desire for a better future.

Joshua and Rebekah Weigel saw an article describing the commendable actions of the Possum Trot neighborhood, which gave them the concept for the movie. They were so moved by the narrative that they felt obliged to share it with more people. The Weigel's, who are renowned for their ability to tell emotionally compelling stories, recognized the possibility of making a movie that would uplift and inspire audiences in addition to providing entertainment.

Understanding the actual events in depth was the first step in the journey. Joshua and Rebekah journeyed to Possum Trot, where they interacted with the locals, heard their tales, and became fully absorbed in their way of life. These conversations greatly aided in the development of the screenplay by supplying a multitude of real-world information that served as the foundation for the movie. From the script to the locations, Weigel's' devotion to authenticity and correctness could be seen in every part of the production, making sure that the movie maintained the essence of Possum Trot.

Joshua and Rebekah worked closely with the Possum Trot community to write the screenplay together. The intention was to craft an engrossing and authentic story that encapsulated the community's resiliency and optimism. The movie's characters were designed to capture the essence of Possum Trot, even though they were based on real people. The community's efforts were greatly aided by the leadership and compassion embodied by Elizabeth Mitchell's Susan Ramsey and Demetrius Grosse's Reverend Martin.

The production phase presented its own set of opportunities and difficulties. Macon, Georgia was selected for filming because of its similarity to Possum Trot and its friendly locals. An $8.5 million budget required careful preparation and ingenuity to manage logistically. To ensure the film's authenticity, the cast and crew frequently went above and above in their persistent efforts to bring the story to life. The finished result, which perfectly embodies Possum Trot, shows how dedicated the creator was to the project.

Securing distribution with Angel Studios was one of the journey's most important turning points. Angel Studios, who are renowned for their dedication to powerful and significant narratives, was the ideal collaborator to introduce "Sound of Hope" to a large audience. Their prior film, "Sound of Freedom," proved to be a hit, proving their capacity to hold audiences' attention and emphasize significant ideas. The choice to premiere the movie on July 4, 2024, was a symbolic one that complemented the themes of hope, unification, and freedom.

A studio-sponsored advance screening of the film will take place on June 19, 2024, two weeks before its official release. This party is a tribute to the teamwork that went into making the movie as well as a celebration of the movie itself. It's a chance to pay tribute to the real-life Possum Trot heroes and tell the world about their experiences.

The process of creating "Sound of Hope: The Story of Possum Trot" was an act of love motivated by a profound regard for the actual events and people who served as inspiration. The movie pays homage to the resilience of the human spirit, the power of community, and the persistent hope that may emerge even in the direst circumstances. In addition to entertaining viewers, we hope this movie will encourage and uplift them by serving as a reminder of the amazing potential for good that every one of us possesses. I hope that the film's portrayal of Possum Trot's narrative will touch you and motivate you to apply its lesson of resiliency and optimism to your own life.

CHAPTER 1

THE ORIGINS OF POSSUM TROT

Historical Context of Possum Trot

The history of Possum Trot, a sleepy rural village in the Southeast of the United States, is as varied and rich as the terrain it lives in. This little hamlet in the middle of Georgia has long been the home of a strong, close-knit community. Possum Trot's beginnings are closely linked to the larger history of the American South, which is marked by the enduring pursuit of racial and social justice, the hardships of Reconstruction, and the legacy of slavery.

It is thought that the term "Possum Trot" originated from the opossums that were formerly common in the area, signifying the ingenuity and flexibility of its people. Early 19th-century residents mostly looking for fertile land for agriculture built the town. It was the perfect place to grow because of the excellent soil and temperate temperature, and cotton quickly took over as the main crop. Possum Trot's economy, like that of much of the South, was largely dependent on the labor of African Americans who were brought into the area as slaves to work on the plantations.

A pivotal moment in Possum Trot's history was the Civil War and the abolition of slavery. There was a significant deal of turbulence and change throughout the Reconstruction era that followed. Despite the harsh realities of segregation and economic hardship, freedmen and their families—

many of whom opted to stay in the area—began to create their villages and churches to start again. During this time, significant social and cultural organizations emerged that would later serve as the cornerstone of the African American community in Possum Trot.

The residents of Possum Trot showed incredible tenacity in the face of systematic prejudice and Jim Crow legislation. They established companies, schools, and churches while cultivating a sense of belonging and unity that would be vital in the years to come. The fight for equality gained fresh impetus during the Civil Rights Movement of the 1950s and 1960s when activists and local leaders played crucial roles in promoting justice and reform.

Key Figures and Community Dynamics

The story of Possum Trot is, at its core, a story of its people. The community has been shaped by numerous individuals who have made significant contributions to its development and spirit. Among these key figures are Reverend Martin, Susan Ramsey, and Donna Martin, each of whom has played a vital role in the town's ongoing narrative.

Reverend Martin

Reverend Martin, a charismatic and dedicated leader, has been a pillar of the Possum Trot community for decades. As the pastor of the town's largest African American church, he has been at the forefront of numerous social and civic initiatives. His efforts to promote education, civil rights, and economic development have left an indelible mark on the town.

Reverend Martin's leadership extends beyond the pulpit. He has been instrumental in organizing voter registration drives, advocating for better public services, and fostering dialogue between different segments of the community. His sermons, often infused with messages of hope, resilience, and justice, have inspired countless individuals to become more active in their community. Under his guidance, the church has become a hub of social activism and support, providing resources and assistance to those in need.

Susan Ramsey

Susan Ramsey is another key figure whose contributions to Possum Trot have been profound. A lifelong resident of the town, Susan has dedicated herself to improving the lives of its residents through education and social work. Her tireless efforts to address issues such as poverty, lack of access to healthcare, and educational disparities have earned her widespread respect and admiration.

Susan's work is deeply personal, rooted in her own experiences growing up in Possum Trot. She understands the challenges faced by many in the community and has used her knowledge and skills to create programs that offer tangible benefits. Her initiatives include after-school tutoring programs, health clinics, and community gardens, all aimed at providing support and opportunities for those who need it most. Susan's ability to connect with people on a personal level has made her a beloved figure in Possum Trot, and her impact on the community is immeasurable.

Donna Martin

Donna Martin, the daughter of Reverend Martin, has followed in her father's footsteps as a community leader and activist. A dynamic and passionate advocate for social justice, Donna has worked tirelessly to address systemic inequalities and promote greater inclusivity in Possum Trot. Her efforts have focused particularly on empowering young people and ensuring that their voices are heard.

Donna's initiatives include youth mentorship programs, leadership development workshops, and advocacy for educational reform. She has also been involved in organizing community events and rallies, bringing attention to critical issues and mobilizing support for change. Donna's commitment to her community is unwavering, and her work continues to inspire new generations of leaders in Possum Trot.

Community Dynamics

Possum Trot community dynamics are typified by a strong sense of camaraderie, reciprocal support, and a steadfast dedication to the well-being of all members. Despite all the difficulties they have encountered, Possum Trot's citizens have constantly banded together to help one another and strive toward shared objectives. The many community organizations and projects that have been founded over the years demonstrate this attitude of solidarity.

The importance of the church is among the most important components of Possum Trot's community dynamics. Historically, religious institutions have played a significant role in the social and cultural life of the community by acting as hubs for social activism and support in addition to being places of worship. The church has served as a pillar of support and encouragement for community organizing and activism.

Another essential element of Possum Trot's community dynamics is education. Many local authorities have made the construction of schools and educational initiatives a top priority because they understand how crucial education is to ending the cycle of poverty and fostering social mobility. In an attempt to enhance educational opportunities, after-school activities, scholarships, and collaborations with nearby schools and institutions have been established.

The Possum Trot community has also placed a strong emphasis on economic development. To develop a more prosperous and sustainable neighborhood, efforts have been made to assist small businesses in the area, generate employment possibilities, and draw in investment. These initiatives have ranged from community redevelopment initiatives to small business development programs.

Additionally, the Possum Trot community is distinguished by its inclusivity and diversity. The community is home to people from many origins and walks of life, despite having a sizable African American population. This diversity is viewed as a positive since it creates a rich cultural tapestry and promotes an atmosphere of respect and understanding between people.

Possum Trot's roots are found in the history and hardships of the American South. The town has evolved from its beginnings as an agricultural hamlet to its current status as a representation of resiliency and hope thanks to the contributions of innumerable people who have devoted their lives to bettering the lives of those who live there.

Important characters in this continuing story, such as Donna Martin, Susan Ramsey, and Reverend Martin, have shown the value of perseverance, leadership, and community spirit.

Possum Trot's dynamics are defined by a strong sense of solidarity, camaraderie, and dedication to the group's welfare. The community's initiatives to advance social justice, economic growth, and education have had a big influence, making the future more prosperous and inclusive for all of its citizens. Possum Trot's narrative is a potent reminder of the value of community, resiliency, and the never-ending pursuit of justice and equality as it develops.

CHAPTER 2

THE STRUGGLE AND RESILIENCE OF THE COMMUNITY

Challenges Faced by the Possum Trot Community

The small, close-knit town of Possum Trot, which is situated in the rural American South, serves as a symbol for the numerous difficulties that similar towns around the country endure. The people who live in Possum Trot, a community that has historically been marginalized and overlooked, have faced numerous challenges that have tried their fortitude and spirit. This chapter explores the major struggles the community has faced and showcases the amazing tales of resiliency and hope that characterize Possum Trot.

Economic Hardships

Economic hardship has been one of Possum Trot's most persistent problems. Agriculture has always been the main industry of the town, providing a living for a large number of its citizens. But changes in the agriculture sector, such as the emergence of massive agribusinesses, have made it harder and harder for small farmers to make a living. Due to the economic pressure, poverty is pervasive and resources are scarce.

The local business closings made the financial problems worse. Many locals found it difficult to make ends meet because there were few job options. The absence of employment opportunities hindered the growth and development of the town as well as the families inside it. A mood of hopelessness spread as companies closed and prospects decreased.

Educational Barriers

Opportunity is fundamentally based on knowledge, but for the kids of Possum Trot, getting a good education has proven to be a major obstacle. Lack of funding for schools, a teacher shortage, and a lack of educational resources have all led to a system that finds it difficult to give children the knowledge and abilities they need to succeed. Low educational attainment keeps the cycle of poverty alive and makes it more difficult for the community to escape economic stagnation.

Furthermore, many young people were forced to leave their homes to seek further education because Possum Trot lacked any nearby higher education facilities. This frequently led to a "brain drain," in which the most intelligent people left the society and did not come back, depleting the pool of knowledgeable and competent citizens who could spearhead future progress.

Social Services and Health

Another crucial area where Possum Trot encountered major obstacles was access to social and medical services. Due to the town's remote location and financial limitations, medical facilities were few and frequently ill-equipped. Long travel times were required for residents to acquire quality healthcare, which was not always possible for those without access to dependable transportation or the financial resources to cover medical costs.

Even though many inhabitants suffered from high levels of stress and trauma, there were particularly few mental health facilities available. The lack of these kinds of support networks made those dealing with mental health problems feel alone and powerless. The community also struggled with drug misuse difficulties, which were made worse by a dearth of social services and support systems to deal with these problems efficiently.

Environmental Challenges

The physical environment of Possum Trot presented its own set of challenges. Natural disasters, such as floods and hurricanes, periodically devastated the area, causing significant damage to homes, infrastructure, and farmland. The community's limited financial resources made recovery efforts slow and arduous, leaving many families struggling to rebuild their lives long after the disasters had passed. The recurring nature of these events meant that the community was often in a state of recovery, which hindered long-term development and progress.

The well-being of the community was also threatened by environmental degradation. The quality of the land and water supplies was impacted by pollution from agricultural practices, biodiversity loss, and soil erosion. In addition to affecting the locals' health, these environmental problems put their main source of income—farming—in jeopardy.

Inspirational Stories of Resilience and Hope

Despite these overwhelming obstacles, the Possum Trot community has continuously shown an amazing ability for hope and resilience. This section features several heartwarming tales that demonstrate the community's unwavering spirit and will to triumph despite hardship.

The Ramsey Initiative

Longtime resident and community activist Susan Ramsey led several efforts to bring Possum Trot back to life. Acknowledging the urgent necessity for educational change, she founded tutoring sessions and after-school programs for kids who were having academic difficulties. These programs gave pupils the much-needed support they needed and greatly raised their academic achievement thanks to donations and volunteers.

Susan also planned neighborhood fundraising events to purchase instructional supplies and upgrade school infrastructure. The town's schools received more funding as a result of her persistent advocacy and efforts to include local and state authorities, which helped to address some of the systemic problems ailing the educational system.

The Outreach Initiatives of Reverend Martin

One of the most important people in Possum Trot, Reverend Martin, was a well-liked character who helped the town come together and support one another. His church developed to become a focal point for outreach initiatives addressing a range of social and economic problems. Seeing the need for work, Reverend Martin organized workshops for job training and collaborated with nearby companies to place citizens in jobs.

The creation of a communal garden was one of the most significant projects. This project functioned as a therapeutic and educational environment in addition to giving fresh vegetables to underprivileged families. By uniting the residents, the garden promoted a feeling of belonging and a common goal. Children were also allowed to learn about agriculture and sustainability through practical experiences.

Donna Martin's Health Advocacy

The wife of Reverend Martin, Donna Martin, a registered nurse, took up the task of enhancing Possum Trot residents' access to healthcare. She set up movable health clinics that made frequent trips to the community, providing free physical examinations, immunizations, and essential medical care. Additionally, Donna started health education initiatives emphasizing healthy lifestyle choices and preventive care.

Knowing how important it is to provide mental health assistance, Donna put in a lot of effort to open a modest counseling center on the church grounds. She enlisted the help of unpaid volunteer therapists and counselors to offer free services to those dealing with mental health problems. Her initiatives greatly lessened the stigma attached to mental health in the community and gave people in need much-needed support.

The Youth's Resilience

Possum Trot's youth have demonstrated incredible fortitude and initiative, frequently volunteering to take on the difficulties facing the neighborhood. Terri, a student in high school, set up a peer mentoring program in which more experienced students helped and guided more junior ones. In addition to raising academic achievement, this program helped the young people develop close relationships and a sense of accountability.

Terri oversaw environmental conservation initiatives and taught her peers the value of safeguarding their natural surroundings. She coordinated efforts to lessen pollution, tree-planting occasions, and clean-up activities. Numerous young citizens were motivated to actively participate in environmental preservation and community well-being by Terri's drive and leadership.

The Role of External Support

The aid and recognition of outside groups and individuals for Possum Trot's potential has also been beneficial to the town's community. Inspired by the locals' tenacity and resolve, nonprofit groups provided funding and resources to assist a range of programs. Possum Trot was frequently visited by volunteers from nearby towns and cities who came to share their skills and lend a hand in community projects.

One especially noteworthy collaboration was with a local institution that offered training courses and workshops to adults and students alike. Along with improving the participants' abilities and knowledge, these programs created new avenues for their professional and personal development.

The Power of Unity and Faith

Possum Trot's tenacity has been based on the strength of unity and faith despite all of these difficulties. The churches in the area were essential in uniting the community by offering both practical and spiritual support. Residents developed a strong sense of camaraderie and support for one another through weekly get-togethers, communal dinners, and prayer groups.

Church-led projects frequently tackled social and economic problems in addition to spiritual ones. For example, churches functioned as shelters and delivery hubs for humanitarian goods during natural catastrophes. The community's resilient character was demonstrated by the sense of cohesion and teamwork throughout these trying times.

Possum Trot's story is one of incredible tenacity and intense difficulty. Notwithstanding considerable obstacles in the areas of healthcare, education, the economy, and the environment, the town has consistently managed to endure and prosper. Possum Trot has been able to overcome hardship and establish a foundation of optimism and resilience thanks to the tireless efforts of people like Susan Ramsey, Donna Martin, Reverend Martin, and the inspirational youth.

Possum Trot has taught us priceless lessons about the power of community, faith, and collective action to bring about dramatic change, even in the face of seemingly insurmountable barriers. Possum Trot's inspirational stories are a ray of hope, showing us all that any community can overcome its obstacles and come out stronger than before if it has perseverance, empathy, and solidarity.

CHAPTER 3

THE CALL TO ACTION

The Pivotal Moments

Moments that act as catalysts for change inspire people and communities to overcome hardship and work toward a better future in every tale of transformation. Such occasions were not random occurrences in Possum Trot; rather, they were momentous occasions that inspired the town's citizens to take action as a group. Possum Trot's transformation from a site of hardship to a ray of hope is evidence of the strength of a strong sense of community, selflessness, and leadership.

The small town of Possum Trot, which is located in the American South, has long struggled with a lack of basic amenities, restricted access to education, and financial difficulties. These difficulties, along with a feeling of abandonment and loneliness, produced a setting that was conducive to hopelessness. But behind all of these hardships was a strong will to succeed and enhance the quality of life for everyone in the community.

Realizing the extent of the community's problems was the first crucial event that created the conditions for transformation. Town meetings hosted by the local church served as a venue for this awakening. Community members recounted their personal stories of struggle, raised concerns, and showed a desire for change as a group during these meetings. The frankness and openness exhibited at these events exposed the breadth of the community's problems and kindled a desire to find answers.

One such gathering—which took place on a steamy July evening—turned out to be pivotal. The cathedral reverberated with the sounds of moving testimony, sobs, and demands for action. Reverend Martin, a warm-hearted and engaging leader who had just been named the community's spiritual advisor, was one of the guests. The accounts of adversity and perseverance touched the heart of Reverend Martin, who listened with great attention. He saw that the community needed more than just spiritual direction; it also required a game plan, a way forward through the perilous path toward a better future.

Reverend Martin's Introduction

Adversity was nothing new to Reverend Martin. Having been raised in a similarly impoverished village, he was aware of the difficulties that

Possum Trot's citizens faced. His struggles and victories along the way to becoming a reverend left him with a strong sense of empathy and a dedication to social justice. Having worked in community organizing for a while and having a strong desire to uplift underprivileged neighborhoods, Reverend Martin was well-suited to guide Possum Trot through its transition.

Establishing a group for community action was Reverend Martin's first step. This group would be in charge of determining the community's most urgent needs and creating plans to meet them. He extended an invitation to join the group to prominent figures in Possum Trot, such as longtime residents, educators, and owners of nearby businesses. Susan Ramsey was one of the people who enthusiastically accepted the invitation. She is a committed educator who has a strong desire to help her pupils and their families.

The Initiatives of Susan Ramsey

Susan Ramsey was a formidable opponent. She was a great gift to the community because of her love of learning and her unshakeable conviction in the potential of every child. She was motivated to change things since she had personally witnessed how poverty and a lack of resources affected her students. Susan provided the committee with a wealth of information regarding the school system and a profound comprehension of the difficulties that the Possum Trot kids encounter.

The community action committee's first significant endeavor was to address the problem of educational disparity. Susan led this initiative, setting up several seminars and tutoring sessions to help students who were having academic difficulties. She enlisted the help of community members, including college students and retired teachers, to act as tutors and mentors. The amount of community members who volunteered their time and knowledge was astounding.

The creation of a community learning center was one of Susan's most ambitious projects. This center became the center of educational activity, housed in a repurposed building provided by a local business owner. It included adult education classes, after-school activities, and a resource library filled with learning resources. In a short time, the learning center came to represent possibilities and optimism, a place where potential might be realized and dreams fostered.

The Ripple Effect of Community Action

The community action committee's efforts started to have an impact on Possum Trot as it carried on with its work. Susan Ramsey and Reverend Martin put forth a lot of effort to make sure their programs were long-lasting and sustainable. They realized that long-term improvements and a fundamental shift in the community's perspective were necessary for real change, not just band-aid fixes.

Promoting a sense of pride and ownership in the community was one of Reverend Martin and Susan's main tactics. They gave citizens the tools they needed to become change agents by encouraging them to participate actively in the initiatives and projects. This strategy assisted in the reconstruction of the community's sense of identity and purpose in addition to guaranteeing the projects' success.

The community's decision to address food insecurity was another crucial turning point in Possum Trot's history. There was a shortage of fresh, wholesome food, and many residents struggled to put food on the table. A community garden initiative was started by the community action group under the direction of Reverend Martin. They turned an empty site into a flourishing garden where locals could cultivate their produce. In addition to serving as a source of fresh vegetables, the garden developed into a hub where neighbors could interact, exchange information, and offer support to one another.

Building Partnerships and Alliances

Beyond Possum Trot's boundaries, Reverend Martin and Susan Ramsey understood the value of forming ties and collaborations. They made efforts to collaborate and get support from nearby communities, small companies, and charitable groups. The success of these programs was greatly dependent on the additional resources, cash, and expertise that these alliances brought in.

A local university was one of these partnerships. Together with the community action group, the university's social work and education departments conducted studies, offered training, and created programs specifically designed to meet Possum Trot's needs. The community's efforts were made more effective by this collaboration, which also gave the participating university students excellent learning opportunities.

The collaboration with nearby companies also turned out to be revolutionary. Numerous companies supplied supplies, gave money, trained individuals for jobs, and offered employment possibilities. These donations enhanced Possum Trot's general standard of living, boosted the local economy, and produced jobs.

Overcoming Obstacles and Honoring Achievements

There were difficulties along the way when Possum Trot was being transformed. Along the journey, Susan Ramsey, Reverend Martin, and the community action committee encountered many challenges. There were moments of uncertainty, obstacles, and opposition from some places. Nevertheless, they continued to advance because of their unshakable dedication to their goal.

Getting enough money for their projects was one of their biggest challenges. There was always a need for more resources, even with the help that partnerships and donations provide. Susan Ramsey and Reverend Martin Ramsey developed skills in grant writing, event planning, and utilizing media attention to draw attention to and support their cause. They were able to expand their projects thanks to the funds and donations they were able to get, demonstrating the value of their tenacity.

Dealing with the distrust and indifference that had crept into some sections of the community was another difficulty. Many inhabitants were disillusioned and cautious of new endeavors as a result of years of neglect and unfulfilled promises. To overcome this obstacle, Reverend Martin and Susan Ramsey kept the lines of communication open, were honest about their goals and development, and acknowledged every accomplishment—no matter how tiny. To make sure that everyone felt included and appreciated, they arranged frequent community meetings, distributed information, and solicited input.

Honoring accomplishments turned became a pillar of their strategy. Every significant occasion was celebrated, from the community learning center's launch to the first harvest from the garden. These occasions not only honored the community's accomplishments and hard work, but they also served as a reminder that change was achievable and that their efforts were having a genuine impact.

The Significance of Spirituality and Faith

The community's spirit and resolve were maintained in large part by faith and spirituality during the process of transition. As a spiritual leader, Reverend Martin took advantage of his position to promote unity, resiliency, and optimism. In his sermons, he emphasized the value of empathy and compassion, the strength of group effort, and the idea that each person can make a positive difference in the world.

The church evolved into more than simply a house of worship; it became a hub for neighborhood organizing, a secure setting for discussion and assistance, and a representation of the community's unwavering faith. Reverend Martin inspired the people and gave them a moral compass for their endeavors by relating spiritual teachings to real-world applications.

Considering the Future

Reverend Martin and Susan Ramsey stayed dedicated to their dream of a thriving, self-sufficient community even as Possum Trot developed and grew. They understood that there was still much to be done and that continuing commitment and flexibility would be needed for the voyage ahead. They were aware of the community's increased resilience and solidarity, nevertheless, and that they had laid a solid foundation.

Their narrative is a potent reminder of what is possible when people band together with a common goal and a strong desire to bring about positive change. It emphasizes the value of community involvement, leadership, and the conviction that any obstacle can be surmounted with tenacity and teamwork.

Possum Trot is a narrative about more than just surviving hardship—it's about the resilience of the human spirit, the strength of community, and the persistent hope that can be found even in the most trying situations. This is a tale that never fails to uplift and remind us that, despite the challenges encountered along the way, heeding the call to action may result in significant transformation and a better future for everybody.

CHAPTER 4

CONCEPTUALIZING THE STORY

Joshua and Rebekah Weigel's Vision for the Film

The dynamic husband-and-wife team of Joshua and Rebekah Weigel set out on a bold endeavor to adapt Possum Trot's inspirational tale for the big screen. Their goal was to make a movie that would inspire and educate viewers about the value of hope, community, and resilience in addition to being a source of entertainment. They were compelled to convey tales of human resilience and unity from the beginning because they had a strong love of storytelling.

The Weigel's were accustomed to powerful narratives. Their earlier films had established them as very skilled detail-oriented directors who had a deep comprehension of human emotions. They sought to explore these topics further in "Sound of Hope: The Story of Possum Trot," using actual occurrences to create an engaging and true story.

Their goal for the movie was very clear: they wanted to make something that offered viewers a glimpse into the lives of the residents of Possum Trot while going beyond simple amusement. This required capturing the essence and spirit of the community in addition to recounting events. They had an idea for a movie that would be real, heartfelt, and able to have a profound effect on viewers.

Writing the Screenplay

Joshua and Rebekah wrote the screenplay for "Sound of Hope: The Story of Possum Trot" out of love. They realized they had to immerse themselves in Possum Trot's universe to give the story properly. This required a great deal of study, numerous interviews, and a careful writing process to guarantee that every detail was true and every character was developed to the fullest.

Research and Immersion

Probably the most important step in drafting a screenplay was the research phase. The Weigels started by researching Possum Trot's past, a tiny but active town with a wealth of anecdotes. They combed through old records, newspaper articles, and video recordings to acquire a thorough grasp of the history and current state of the city.

However, the reach of books and articles was limited. The Weigels decided to travel to Possum Trot to fully grasp the spirit of the town. They lived among the people for a few weeks, watching their daily activities and hearing their experiences. They were able to personally witness the struggles and victories of the community thanks to this immersion method, which gave them priceless insights into their work.

Joshua and Rebekah interviewed some important community members during their visit, including longtime residents, prominent individuals in the town, and those who directly participated in the events that served as the inspiration for the movie. The screenplay was meticulously scrutinized to ensure that the voices of Possum Trot were accurately portrayed by the meticulous recording, transcription, and analysis of these talks.

Creating the Story

Equipped with an abundance of research materials, the Weigels set about the difficult work of writing the screenplay. They began by outlining the main plot points and character arcs in a thorough outline. Their objective was to balance dramatic elements with the unvarnished reality of the community's experiences to create a narrative that was both captivating and truthful to the original story.

One of the main difficulties they encountered was fitting a convoluted and intricate tale into a two-hour movie. Possum Trot activities took place over many years and involved many people, each with their own distinct experiences and viewpoints. The Weigels addressed this by concentrating on a small number of key characters whose narratives captured the larger concepts they wished to express.

Character Formation

These characters required careful development. The Weigels wanted to develop multifaceted characters that could appeal to a broad audience while yet being true to the real people on whom they were based. They included characteristics, eccentricities, and motivations in the characters that accurately represented the experiences of the Possum Trot locals by heavily drawing from their observations and interviews.

Susan Ramsey, portrayed by Elizabeth Mitchell, became a pivotal character in the movie. Susan's persona—a resolute and empathetic leader—was modeled after several actual people who were instrumental in the community's attempts to triumph over hardship. She was portrayed by the

Weigels as a woman motivated by a strong sense of obligation to her community, a ray of hope and resiliency.

Another important role was Demetrius Grosse's portrayal of Reverend Martin. His persona was designed to represent the moral and spiritual core of Possum Trot, a community leader who persevered through great adversity with unwavering faith and resolve. The Weigels investigated questions of faith, leadership, and the effectiveness of group action through Reverend Martin.

Pastor Mark, played by Joshua Weigel, and Donna Martin, portrayed by Nika King, were both essential characters in the story. Pastor Mark symbolized the difficulties and rewards of guiding a community through difficult times, while Donna was created to represent the tenacity and fortitude of Possum Trot's women.

Diaana Babnicova's portrayal of young Terri was a composite figure who stood in for Possum Trot's youth. The movie showed the aspirations and hardships, as well as the victories, of the younger generation as seen through her eyes.

Keeping Fiction and Facts in Check

The Weigels acknowledged the necessity for artistic license to improve the dramatic impact of the story, even as they were dedicated to remaining faithful to the facts. This required combining fictional and real-world events, developing composite characters, and shortening timelines. Their objective was to preserve the film's essential authenticity while making it both captivating and emotionally impactful.

For instance, to increase the emotional tension and cohesiveness of the story, several incidents were dramatized. The dialogue was written to capture the spirit of the characters' experiences and successfully express their feelings. The Weigels took care to find a middle ground so that the narrative's integrity wouldn't be jeopardized by these artistic choices.

Themes and Messages

"Sound of Hope: The Story of Possum Trot" is primarily a movie about hope, community, and resiliency. The Weigels were committed to including these ideas within the storyline and emphasizing them throughout the script. Every character and story point was created to reiterate these key ideas, resulting in a coherent and powerful narrative.

The way the characters handled hardship showed resilience and their capacity to go on in the face of enormous obstacles. The strength that results from unity and solidarity was demonstrated by the community's combined efforts. The movie made a strong point on how important it is to stick together in the face of adversity through trials and victories.

Another important element was hope. The Weigels aimed to demonstrate that hope can be a beacon of light, even amid the direst circumstances. The protagonists' steadfast faith in a brighter future and their resolve to bring about constructive change reflected this. The movie wanted viewers to go away feeling hopeful and believing in the goodness and resiliency of people.

The Writing Process

There were multiple drafts and adjustments made during the actual writing process. The Weigels would write, edit, and rewrite the script several times over to make sure it lived up to their exacting standards. To get the greatest result, they worked closely together, frequently disputing and discussing different sections of the script.

They also asked dependable coworkers and business experts for input, adding helpful critiques to improve the script. This iterative process was essential to creating a polished and captivating story while maintaining Possum Trot's essence.

Challenges and Triumphs

The screenplay writing process wasn't without its difficulties. It was a difficult effort to strike a balance between the necessity for dramatic storytelling and the obligation to authentically reflect actual events. The Weigels experienced periods of uncertainty and exasperation as they considered the scope of the tale they were narrating.

There were, yet, also times of victory. Deeply satisfying experiences were seeing the characters come to life on the paper, encapsulating Possum Trot, and creating an interesting yet poignant story. The Weigels' commitment to excellence and diligence paid off, producing a screenplay that was a genuine labor of love.

When Joshua and Rebekah Weigel conceived "Sound of Hope: The Story of Possum Trot," they wanted to make a movie that went beyond a simple recounting of events. Their goal was to convey the perseverance, hope, and force of group action while capturing the essence of a community. They created a screenplay that was both captivating and faithful to Possum Trot's spirit by doing a great deal of research, writing carefully, and having a strong commitment to authenticity.

Their love for storytelling and desire to inspire audiences drove them through many obstacles and victories along the concept to script process. The outcome was a screenplay that powerfully expressed the human spirit's enduring fortitude while simultaneously telling the story of Possum Trot.

CHAPTER 5

CASTING AND CHARACTER DEVELOPMENT

Selection of Actors

Sound of Hope: The Story of Possum Trot underwent a careful and deliberate casting process. The film's writers, Joshua, and Rebekah Weigel, knew that casting performers who could authentically portray the nuanced and inspirational individuals at the center of the narrative would be critical to its success. This chapter explores the process of choosing the main cast, which includes Elizabeth Mitchell, Demetrius Grosse, Nika King, Joshua Weigel, and Diaana Babnicova. It also looks at the characters they played and the extensive preparations they underwent.

Susan Ramsey, played by Elizabeth Mitchell

Elizabeth Mitchell was an obvious option for Susan Ramsey because of her many roles in The Expanse and Lost. Mitchell was a wonderful fit for Susan because of her ability to portray bravery, vulnerability, and unshakable perseverance. Susan was modeled from actual Possum Trot advocates.

Mitchell impressed the casting directors not only with her acting skills but also with her sincere interest in the narrative. She expressed her admiration for the work these people accomplished, spending hours talking about the real-life sources of inspiration for Susan Ramsey. Her screen test demonstrated this enthusiasm, as she portrayed Susan's compassion and resiliency in a nuanced manner.

Reverend Martin, played by Demetrius Grosse

Renowned actor Demetrius Grosse, who starred in Lovecraft Country and Fear the Walking Dead, gave Reverend Martin a rich depth. The story revolves around Reverend Martin, a man whose faith and leadership inspire the neighborhood to undergo radical change.

After a thorough search for an actor who could embody the grace and gravity of Reverend Martin, Grosse made his casting decision. His audition was strong, demonstrating both his capacity to hold an audience's attention and his profound empathy. Because of his theater training, Grosse was able to give Reverend Martin a dynamic presence that connected with the entire crew and actors.

Donna Martin, played by Nika King

Nika King, who won praise for her performance in Euphoria, was chosen to play Donna Martin, the Reverend Martin's resolute and encouraging wife. King's portrayal of Donna, who stands in for the core of her family and the town, required him to strike a balance between sensitivity and strength.

King's audition demonstrated her ability to vividly depict complex personalities. She gave Donna a warmth and resiliency that helped people relate to her right away. King approached the role from all angles; she took the time to learn about Donna's upbringing, her goals, and the complex dynamics of her relationship with Reverend Martin.

Pastor Mark, played by Joshua Weigel

As Pastor Mark, Joshua Weigel stepped both in front of and behind the camera. Weigel's desire to preserve the story's authenticity and his connection to the tale motivated him to take on this position.

Pastor Mark is an important figure in the community because he acts as a mediator and mentor to many factions. Weigel was able to give Pastor Mark a distinct depth because of his deep comprehension of the story's themes. Although juggling two roles—director and actor—required a careful balance, his love for the project made sure that each was performed to the highest standard.

Terri (Diaana Babnicova)

Rising actress Diaana Babnicova, who has acted in indie films and television before, was chosen to play young Terri, a character whose path embodies the potential and hope of the Possum Trot community. Babnicova's fresh enthusiasm and poignant performance were essential to making Terri's tale come to life.

Babnicova made a memorable audition throughout the casting process. She showed a natural ability to portray Terri's hardships and victories, encapsulating the spirit of a person who represents Possum Trot's future. Babnicova was a fantastic addition to the group because of her new outlook and early commitment to the part.

A Comprehensive Look into Actor Preparation and Character Portrayals

Susan Ramsey, played by Elizabeth Mitchell

With a great sense of responsibility, Mitchell took on the character of Susan Ramsey. She conducted in-depth research and spoke with the real-life inspirations of the character Susan to depict her accurately. Mitchell went to Possum Trot and spoke with local leaders, learning about their struggles and achievements.

To improve Susan's accent and mannerisms, Mitchell also worked extensively with a dialect coach as part of her preparation. She became fully engaged in the community, going to church and other events, to gain a deeper understanding of the setting Susan would be living in daily. Her performance was praised for its honesty and emotional depth, demonstrating the fruit of her effort.

Mitchell was well-known on set for her exacting attention to detail. She frequently conferred with Joshua Weigel over scene details to make sure that Susan's spirit was faithfully captured in each shot. Her portrayal of Susan Ramsey turned into a defining feature of the movie, providing an emotional and strong performance that grounded the narrative.

Reverend Martin, played by Demetrius Grosse

Reverend Martin was portrayed by Grosse with a strong sense of empathy and a commanding presence. He researched the lives of community organizers and civil rights leaders for months to prepare for the part. To create a speaking style that embodied Reverend Martin's charisma and leadership, Grosse worked with a vocal coach.

Grosse interacted with pastors who had spearheaded comparable initiatives and frequently attended church services in an attempt to take on the moral and spiritual weight of Reverend Martin. He observed their interactions with their congregations, their body language, and their preaching techniques. Grosse was able to offer sermons with a captivating realism that struck a deep chord with the audience because of this research.

Grosse prepared physically as well, following Reverend Martin's regimen that reflected his strict way of living. By treating the role holistically, Grosse was able to fully embody Reverend Martin and provide a portrayal that was both profoundly human and inspirational.

Donna Martin, played by Nika King

Nika King had to strike a careful balance between sensitivity and strength in her portrayal of Donna Martin. King investigated the special difficulties and benefits associated with the job by fully immersing herself in the life of a pastor's wife. She gained insight into the daily lives and sacrifices of women who had gone through comparable circumstances by speaking with them.

To prepare, King studied Donna's past and her connection with Reverend Martin in great detail. She worked closely with Demetrius Grosse to create a compelling and lively on-screen duo. Their scenes together demonstrated the close relationship and respect that Donna and Reverend Martin shared, and this chemistry was clear to see.

King was equally committed to being truthful in her physical representation. She made sure Donna's presence seemed authentic to the time and place by dressing and acting in a manner consistent with the period. Donna Martin was brought to life by her nuanced portrayal, which emphasized the character's tenacity and unfailing devotion to her family and community.

Pastor Mark, played by Joshua Weigel

Joshua Weigel faced particular difficulties in his dual capacity as director and actor, but his strong emotional attachment to the narrative enhanced his portrayal of Pastor Mark. Weigel studied the characters and the script in great detail to prepare for the part. He took inspiration from people who had healed divisions within their communities, both historical and modern.

Weigel's interpretation of Pastor Mark was influenced by both his own life experiences and his comprehension of the character's essential function in the story. He kept a clear picture of the story's emotional center, which helped him balance his directing and acting roles. Weigel was able to give a performance that was both perceptive and powerful because of this dual viewpoint.

Weigel's cooperation with the actors and staff on the set created a friendly and helpful atmosphere. He captured the essence of a character that acts as a guiding light in the plot with his depiction of Pastor Mark, which was characterized by a calm strength and a strong feeling of empathy.

Terri (Diaana Babnicova)

Diaana Babnicova's youthful excitement and commitment to sincerity were evident in her preparation for the role of Terri. As a young actress, Babnicova gave the role a new angle by using her personal experiences to guide Terri's path.

Babnicova worked on Terri's past and goals for a long time, developing her character. She was able to establish a strong connection with the role by taking part in improvisation and emotional truth-focused workshops and rehearsals. Babnicova was able to give a powerful and poignant performance because of her preparation.

To accurately portray Terri's challenges and achievements, Babnicova spent time interacting with kids and families from comparable backgrounds. She gained an understanding of

Terri's struggles and the hope that kept her going via this immersion. In the movie, Babnicova's portrayal of Terri turns into a ray of hope, personifying Possum Trot's future.

Collaborative Character Development

One of the key elements of Sound of Hope: The Story of Possum Trot was the collaborative nature of the character-building process. Joshua and Rebekah Weigel's performances were carefully crafted by the cast members to make sure they were authentic and relatable to the viewer.

Workshops and Rehearsals

To develop a thorough grasp of the characters and their interactions, some workshops and rehearsals were held as part of the preparation process. The performers were able to experiment with various methods and interpretations during these sessions as they dug deeper into their roles.

The cast participated in character-building activities like scene studies and improvisations during these seminars. The performers were able to gain a solid understanding of the dynamics and motivations of their characters thanks to these exercises. Open communication and creative inquiry were fostered by the collaborative atmosphere, which produced performances with a great depth of layers.

Participation in the Community

Interacting with the Possum Trot community was an essential component of the planning process. To further comprehend the real-life setting of the story, the cast members went on visits, went to local events, and engaged in conversation with the people living there. Their performances gained more sincerity and insightful information from this interaction.

The performers were able to understand the subtleties of the story and the tenacity of the people who inspired it through their contact with members of the community. Their representations were informed by these experiences, which enabled them to authentically convey a sense of location and community on television.

Sound of Hope: The Story of Possum Trot involved a collaborative and immersive casting and character creation process. A strong cast that brought the drama to life included Elizabeth Mitchell, Demetrius Grosse, Nika King, Joshua Weigel, and Diaana Babnicova, each of whom brought special skills and viewpoints to their roles.

With meticulous planning, extensive community involvement, and a dedication to genuineness, the ensemble gave performances that perfectly encapsulated Possum Trot. Their performances not only paid tribute to the story's real-life sources of inspiration, but they also struck a deep chord with viewers, making Sound of Hope: The Story of Possum Trot an engrossing and poignant cinematic experience.

CHAPTER 6

FILMING IN MACON, GEORGIA

Choice of Location and Its Significance

An important choice that gave the production more depth and authenticity was to film "Sound of Hope: The Story of Possum Trot" in Macon, Georgia. Macon, a historically significant and charming Southern city, made the ideal setting for a drama about a close-knit society dealing with serious issues. The village was a perfect place to film because of its unique architectural style, vibrant culture, and strong sense of community, all of which reflected the spirit of Possum Trot.

Because of its historical value and the preservation of buildings from the 19th and early 20th centuries, Macon provided an authentic and visually appealing environment. The filmmakers aimed to portray the spirit of a community in which contemporary hardships and resiliency coexist with history and tradition. The city's historic neighborhoods, with their traditional Southern architecture, gave the movie an air of timeless elegance and helped to set the narrative in a familiar and approachable world.

Furthermore, the film's fundamental themes of hope and communal spirit resonated with Macon's cultural landscape, which is marked by a lively arts scene and rich musical tradition. The story of the movie was enhanced by the city's enduring traditions of gospel, blues, and soul music, which produced an emotional undertone. This cultural background gave the narrative a more authentic touch by offering both a visual and an emotional context.

Macon's significance went beyond its physical characteristics. The participation of the community in the filming process fostered a sincere feeling of communal spirit and cooperation. Locals were keen to get involved, whether as project supporters, extras, or backstage crew members. This interaction further blurred the boundaries between the plot and its environment by fostering a social atmosphere that echoed the themes of the movie. The real-life Macon community contributed its own stories, experiences, and spirit to the fictional story, giving the movie a more personal touch.

Behind the Scenes of the Production

"Sound of Hope: The Story of Possum Trot" was a thrilling and difficult filming project in Macon. The production crew overcame many logistical, artistic, and technological obstacles with a collaborative and innovative mindset.

Pre-Production and Setting Up

Preparing for a seamless filming procedure required a lot of work in advance. Weeks were spent in Macon by location scouts finding the ideal locations to replace the fictitious Possum Trot. Every setting, from the picturesque outskirts to the quaint city, was carefully selected to guarantee that it would add to the genuine atmosphere of the movie.

Securing licenses and working with local officials was one of the main pre-production obstacles. To guarantee that filming could take place without significantly interfering with inhabitants' daily lives, the production team maintained close communication with Macon city officials. The smoother logistics throughout the filming were made possible by the strong relationship that this collaboration helped to establish with the local population.

The Filming Process

The production crew put in a lot of overtime throughout the three months of real filming in Macon to make the script come to life. Every day brought new difficulties, but it also brought back special moments that demonstrated the commitment and enthusiasm of all those engaged.

Challenges in Logistics

Getting used to the erratic weather was one of the first big obstacles. Although the fall weather in Macon is usually warm, there are erratic weather patterns that include unexpected downpours and temperature swings. The team had to be flexible and adaptable due to the weather variables; they frequently had to reschedule scenes or make last-minute changes to the filming schedule. Notwithstanding these difficulties, the erratic weather also produced a few really lovely moments that improved the visual appeal of the movie.

Organizing the crew and cast's transportation was another logistical problem. Making sure that everyone was in the right place at the right time, among a vast cast of performers, directors, camera operators, and support personnel, was a difficult assignment. To keep everything moving along smoothly, the production crew used a fleet of local transportation providers and a rigorous scheduling system. The smooth running and effective execution of the filming process depended on this careful coordination.

Creative Challenges and Solutions

Ensuring that the film's visual style stayed constant while conveying Macon's soul posed a huge creative hurdle. Under the direction of the director of photography, the cinematography team had to strike a balance between the story's thematic themes and the natural beauty of the setting. To provide a cozy and engaging watching experience, they used a range of methods, such as handheld camera work and natural lighting. This strategy emphasized the individuals' emotional experiences in addition to highlighting Macon's physical attractiveness.

The depiction of the resiliency and spirit of the community presented another creative challenge. The filmmakers used real-life facts and personal accounts from Macon locals to accurately depict this. Local extras appeared in a number of the scenes, lending the story more depth and realism. To give the Possum Trot community a more genuine and passionate representation, the production crew also took inspiration from regional traditions and customs and incorporated them into the movie.

Memorable Moments

The cast and crew all agreed that many special moments came to mind during the filming process. These instances brought to light not only the difficulties encountered but also the victories and delights had along the journey.

One scenario that took place in a nearby church stands out in particular. Elizabeth Mitchell gave a moving monologue about resiliency and optimism while portraying Susan Ramsey. Both the crew and the actors were moved to tears by the depth of emotion in her performance. This moment was a game-changer for the production since it captured the basic idea of the movie and established a high bar for the other scenes.

Filming a scene of a neighborhood gathering was another amazing experience. Participation was open to locals, and there was a genuine sense of happiness and unity in the air. Traditional Southern music and dancing were used in the scene, which produced a bright and joyous atmosphere. The actual essence of the neighborhood was captured by the filmmakers, who could feel the enthusiasm on set. This sequence evolved into a celebration of the Macon community in real life as well as the narrative being portrayed.

Long-lasting memories were also forged by the cast's encounters with the locals. The actor who played Reverend Martin, Demetrius Grosse, frequently spent time getting to know the people in the town so that he could include their tales in his acting. These exchanges gave his portrayal of the character more nuance and realism. The cast and the locals' mutual regard and appreciation for one another created a cooperative and encouraging atmosphere in production.

Technical Difficulties

There were additional difficulties posed by the technical requirements of filming in Macon. The production crew had to deal with the restrictions of filming in a tiny city, such as having little access to upscale equipment and facilities. The crew frequently had to use creativity to overcome these obstacles, making use of available local resources and adjusting to environmental restrictions.

Ensuring constant sound quality was a major technical problem. Filming in an urban setting required adjusting to background noise from nearby businesses, pedestrians, and vehicles. The sound crew minimized background noise and captured high-quality audio by using cutting-edge recording techniques and equipment. Retakes and more sound editing were frequently needed for this in post-production, but the work was crucial to preserving the film's high caliber.

Another technical challenge was lighting, especially for scenes set at night. The crew had to improvise, using a combination of rented lights and natural sources due to Macon's limited supply of professional lighting equipment. The cinematography crew used their creativity to experiment with various setups until they found the ideal balance to produce the intended lighting effects. These efforts paid off, producing striking visual sequences that elevated the overall aesthetic of the movie.

Participation and Assistance from the Community

The Macon community's assistance was crucial to the filming process's success. Businesses and locals went above and beyond to make accommodations for the shoot, providing everything from food services to lodging for the actors and crew. This assistance not only made filming more manageable logistically, but it also fostered a feeling of appreciation and community.

One of the production team's local fundraisers was one of the highlights of community involvement. The event was designed to help neighborhood nonprofits and charities give back to the community. It included a Q&A session with the cast and crew and a sneak peek at a few sequences from the movie. The fundraiser was a huge success, bringing in a substantial amount of money and strengthening the relationship between the filmmakers and the local community.

A distinctive element was also brought to the production by the participation of nearby educational institutions and schools. Visitors from Macon's schools were welcomed to the set, where they were able to observe the filmmaking process directly from the source. Through seminars and interactive sessions with the actors and crew, these trips allowed students to learn about a variety of film production-related topics. For many, the high point of this educational outreach was that it encouraged a new generation of aspiring filmmakers and storytellers.

The process of filming "Sound of Hope: The Story of Possum Trot" in Macon, Georgia, was filled with obstacles, ingenuity, and teamwork. The film's realism and depth were greatly enhanced by the choice of setting, and the cast, crew, and community worked hard behind the scenes to make the story come to life.

Resilience and creativity were displayed in the face of logistical and creative obstacles encountered during the filming process, culminating in a film that not only tells a gripping story but also honors the spirit of the town that served as its inspiration.

Remarkable incidents that transpired both on and off set highlighted the enthusiasm and commitment of all those involved, leaving a lasting impression that went beyond the screen.

The process of filming in Macon served as a monument to the strength of community, teamwork, and the common goal of narrating a tale that is both hopeful and true. The making of "Sound of Hope: The Story of Possum Trot" is a moving reminder of both the lasting resilience of the human spirit and the transformational power of film as the movie prepares for its theatrical debut.

CHAPTER 7

BUDGET AND PRODUCTION LOGISTICS

Managing an $8.5 Million Budget

Managing a film budget is a complex and multifaceted process that requires meticulous planning, careful allocation of resources, and constant monitoring to ensure that every dollar is spent effectively. For "Sound of Hope: The Story of Possum Trot," the budget of $8.5 million was a significant but manageable sum that allowed the filmmakers to bring their vision to life while maintaining financial discipline.

Initial Budget Planning

The process started with the first budget planning stage, during which the producers and directors, Joshua and Rebekah Weigel, laid out the project's general financial strategy. This included dividing the money into pre-production, production, post-production, and distribution divisions. Every category was then broken down into individual line items, including marketing, special effects, venues, equipment, salaries, costumes, and more.

Making a thorough budget proposal and presenting it to studios and possible investors was essential at this planning stage. The projected expenses and the clever financial management that would guarantee the project stayed below budget were emphasized in this proposal. The Weigels had been in the film business before, so they knew how important it was to have reasonable expectations and contingencies to cover unforeseen costs.

Pre-Production Costs

Pre-production is where significant groundwork is laid, and expenses start to accrue even before the cameras begin rolling. In this phase, a portion of the budget was allocated to:

Script Development and Rights Acquisition: While the story was inspired by true events, the rights to certain aspects and consultations with the real-life subjects and communities involved needed to be secured.

Casting: Finding the right actors for key roles was crucial. Casting directors were hired, auditions were conducted, and contracts were negotiated. For "Sound of Hope," attracting established actors like Elizabeth Mitchell and Demetrius Grosse required competitive salaries, which were a significant part of the budget.

Location Scouting and Permits: Filming in Macon, Georgia, required scouting various locations that would authentically represent Possum Trot. This involved travel expenses, location fees, and obtaining necessary filming permits.

Production Design: Designing sets, planning costumes, and gathering props that would faithfully recreate the era and setting of the story.

Production Costs

The production phase is typically the most expensive, encompassing a wide range of activities and resources necessary to shoot the film. Key production expenses included:

Salaries and Crew Costs: This was one of the largest budget items. It included payments for the cast, director, producers, cinematographers, sound engineers, makeup artists, costume designers, and a host of other essential crew members. Union regulations and fair compensation practices were strictly adhered to.

Equipment Rental: High-quality cameras, lighting, and sound equipment were rented for the shoot. Ensuring top-tier equipment was vital for achieving the desired cinematic quality.

Set Construction and Art Department: Significant funds were allocated to building sets that were historically accurate and visually compelling. The art department played a crucial role in creating immersive environments that transported audiences to Possum Trot.

Transportation and Accommodation: Moving the cast and crew to various locations, providing lodging, and ensuring their well-being were logistical challenges that required careful planning and significant financial resources.

Catering and Craft Services: Keeping the cast and crew well-fed and hydrated during long shooting days was essential for maintaining morale and productivity.

Special Effects and Stunts: Any required special effects or stunts were planned, with safety measures and insurance taking a substantial part of the budget.

Post-Production Costs

Post-production is where the film truly comes together, and significant resources are allocated to this phase to ensure the final product meets the highest standards. Key areas of expenditure included:

Editing: Hiring experienced editors to assemble the footage, refine the narrative, and ensure seamless transitions was crucial. This also involved multiple editing suites and software licenses.

Sound Design and Mixing: Creating an immersive soundscape requires the talents of skilled sound designers and mixers. This also included recording any necessary ADR (Automated Dialogue Replacement) and sound effects.

Music: Composing and recording the film's score, as well as securing rights for any additional music used, was a significant expense.

Visual Effects: While "Sound of Hope" primarily focused on a grounded, realistic portrayal, any necessary visual effects needed to be top-notch and integrated seamlessly with the live-action footage.

Color Grading: Ensuring visual consistency and enhancing the mood through color grading requires specialized professionals and equipment.

Marketing and Distribution: Although this falls slightly outside traditional post-production, planning the marketing strategy and securing distribution channels were critical. This included creating promotional materials, trailers, and advertising campaigns.

Key Production Roles and Their Contributions

The success of "Sound of Hope: The Story of Possum Trot" was not only due to financial planning but also to the dedication and expertise of the production team. Here are some of the key roles and their contributions to the film:

Director: Joshua Weigel

As the director, Joshua Weigel was the creative force behind the film. He was responsible for:

Vision and Direction: Setting the overall vision for the film, from the visual style to the pacing and tone.

Working with Actors: Guiding performances to ensure that each actor brought their character to life authentically and compellingly.

Overseeing Production: Coordinating with all departments to ensure that the film stayed on track and that his vision was realized.

Producer: Rebekah Weigel

Rebekah Weigel played a crucial role in managing the production's logistics and ensuring everything ran smoothly. Her responsibilities included:

Budget Management: Keeping a close eye on expenditures and ensuring the project stays within budget.

Scheduling: Coordinating the shooting schedule to maximize efficiency and minimize downtime.

Problem Solving: Addressing any issues that arose during production, from logistical challenges to interpersonal conflicts.

Cinematographer: Benji Bakshi Sean Patrick Kirby

The cinematographer, also known as the Director of Photography (DP), was responsible for the visual aspects of the film. Their contributions included:

Visual Style: Crafting the film's visual aesthetic, including lighting, framing, and camera movement.

Camera Operation: Supervising the camera crew and ensuring that each shot was captured perfectly.

Technical Expertise: Selecting and managing the camera equipment and ensuring that technical aspects like exposure and focus are precise.

Production Designer: Debbie DeVilla

The production designer was essential in creating the world of Possum Trot. Their responsibilities included:

Set Design: Designing and overseeing the construction of sets that accurately represent the story's setting and period.

Art Direction: Managing the art department to ensure that all visual elements, from props to locations, contributed to the film's authenticity.

Costume Designer: Ellen Falguiere

The costume designer played a key role in defining the characters visually. Their work involved:

Costume Design: Designing and sourcing costumes that reflect the characters' personalities and the film's period.

Fittings and Adjustments: Ensuring that each actor's costume fit perfectly and allowed them to perform comfortably.

Editor: David Andalman

The editor's role was critical in shaping the final product. Their contributions included:

Assembling Footage: Piecing together the various takes and scenes to form a coherent and engaging narrative.

Pacing and Timing: Ensuring that the film's pacing kept audiences engaged and that each scene transitioned smoothly.

Collaborating with the Director: Working closely with Joshua Weigel to ensure that the final cut matched his vision.

Sound Designer: Jeremy Rock

Sound design was essential for creating an immersive experience. The sound designer's responsibilities included:

Sound Effects and Foley: Creating and recording sound effects that added depth and realism to the film.

Dialogue and ADR: Ensuring that all dialogue was clear and any additional recordings were seamlessly integrated.

Sound Mixing: Balancing all audio elements to create a cohesive soundscape.

Composer: Joshua Weigel, Rebekah Weigel

The composer was responsible for the film's musical score. Their contributions included:

Scoring: Composing original music that underscored the film's emotional beats and themes.

Recording: Working with musicians and sound engineers to record the score.

Integration: Collaborating with the sound designer and editor to ensure the music complemented the film perfectly.

Marketing and Distribution Team

The marketing and distribution team played a vital role in ensuring the film reached its audience. Their work involved:

Marketing Strategy: Develop a comprehensive marketing plan that includes trailers, posters, social media campaigns, and press releases.

Distribution Deals: Securing deals with theaters and streaming platforms to maximize the film's reach.

Premiere and Screenings: Organizing advance screenings and the premiere to generate buzz and attract media attention.

Managing the $8.5 million budget for "Sound of Hope: The Story of Possum Trot" required a blend of financial acumen, strategic planning, and the collaborative efforts of a dedicated production team. Each team member, from the director to the sound designer, played a crucial role in bringing the film to life, ensuring that the story of Possum Trot was told with the authenticity, emotional depth, and visual richness it deserved. Through meticulous budget management and the contributions of talented professionals, the film not only stayed within its financial constraints but also achieved a level of quality that resonated with audiences and critics alike.

CHAPTER 8

DIRECTING THE VISION

Joshua Weigel's Directorial Approach

The path taken by Joshua Weigel in directing "Sound of Hope: The Story of Possum Trot" is evidence of his love of narrative and commitment to making a picture that has a profound impact on viewers. Weigel took a comprehensive approach to directing this movie, relying on a strong sense of authenticity, a collaborative attitude, and a thorough comprehension of the story.

One way to characterize Weigel's directing style is immersive and character-driven. He thinks that stories can change and unite people. With "Sound of Hope," Weigel aimed to produce a movie that conveyed the spiritual and emotional core of the community's journey in addition to presenting the events of Possum Trot. He intended to evoke in the audience the hardships, victories, and unshakable hope that defined the true tale.

Weigel was heavily involved in every stage of the film's development from the beginning. He spoke with members of the Possum Trot community, studied the actual events that served as the basis for the novel, and fully immersed himself in the social and cultural milieu of the area over several months. His ability to direct with honesty and respect for the genuine individuals whose lives were being portrayed on television was made possible by this in-depth insight.

Weigel's meticulous approach to directing "Sound of Hope" was another distinguishing feature. He carefully thought out every scene, taking into account each component's role in the larger story as well as its aesthetic composition. Weigel believed that directing was about creating an experience that would stick with audiences long after they left the theater, not just narrating a story.

Collaborations

One of the defining features of Weigel's directorial approach was his emphasis on collaboration. He believed that a film of this magnitude could only be successful if everyone involved was fully committed to bringing the story to life. From the cast to the crew, Weigel fostered a collaborative environment where everyone's input was valued and respected.

Collaborating with the Writers:

Joshua worked extensively with co-writer Rebekah Weigel to make sure the screenplay was truthful to the historical story while yet being entertaining. The writers worked closely together throughout the writing process, constantly exchanging ideas and criticism. Joshua's approach to directing was informed by the screenplay, which in turn informed his directorial vision. This repeated procedure contributed to building a solid cinematic basis.

Building the Cast:

Another essential component of Weigel's teamwork was casting. He thought that the characters could be given greater depth and authenticity by the right performers, which would increase the story's impact and relatability. When Elizabeth Mitchell was chosen to play Susan Ramsey, she gave a subtle performance that brought out the compassion and resiliency of the role. In his role as Reverend Martin, Demetrius

Grosse personified the fortitude and tenacity of a civic leader. With powerful performances, Nika King, Joshua Weigel, and Diaana Babnicova also brought their roles to life.

Weigel worked carefully with each actor to make sure they were aware of the motivations and histories of their respective roles. He fostered a sense of ownership and involvement in the plot by encouraging them to apply their interpretations to the roles. The success of the movie was largely due to the director and performers' working relationship, which made it possible for performances to be both genuine and emotionally impactful.

Engaging with the Crew:

Weigel worked with the entire team in addition to the actors. He collaborated closely with production designers, cinematographers, and other important team members to make sure that his vision was reflected in every area of the movie. Cinematographer Benji Bakshi and Sean Patrick Kirby collaborated with Weigel to craft a visually striking and thematically fitting look, which was crucial in establishing the film's visual language.

Collaboration was also crucial in the field of production design. The crew put forth a great deal of effort and meticulous attention to detail to reproduce Possum Trot's environment. Everything, down to the smallest props, was carefully chosen to mirror the real-life village, including the building architecture.

Creative Decisions

The film's story, aesthetic, and emotional tone were all molded by the creative choices made by Weigel to realize his vision as a filmmaker.

Visual Design:

The film's visual aesthetic was one of the most important creative choices. Weigel intended "Sound of Hope" to have a unique aesthetic that would improve the narrative. He chose a naturalistic look, making use of handheld cameras and ambient light to produce a close-knit atmosphere. With this strategy, the audience was given the impression that they were a member of the community and were experiencing the events with the characters.

There was also thought put into the color scheme. Together, Weigel and the cinematographer created a color scheme that represented the characters' emotional development. Darker, muted hues were used in scenes that showed the community's problems, while warm, earthy tones were used to portray a sense of hope and perseverance.

Story Structure:

The "Sound of Hope" narrative structure was thoughtfully designed to strike a balance between the story of the larger community and the portrayal of individual persons. Weigel decided to employ a nonlinear structure, fusing current events with flashbacks. This strategy maintained the attention on the protagonists' continuous trip while enabling the audience to comprehend Possum Trot's background and context.

Weigel also took the imaginative step of telling the story from several points of view. His ability to provide voice to various characters allowed him to portray a more thorough and nuanced picture of the community's experience. This decision enhanced the narrative while highlighting the journey's communal aspect and highlighting the fact that Possum Trot was a story about a whole community rather than simply a select few people.

Sound and Music:

Sound and music were very important in determining the film's emotional tone. Weigel collaborated with composer Joshua Weigel and Rebekah Weigel to produce a soundtrack that would support the narrative and elicit the right feelings. The movie's soundtrack was thoughtfully included, with distinct themes connected to various characters and scenes. By emphasizing the narrative's emotional highs and lows, this strategy enhanced the audience's immersion and impact.

Sound design held equal significance. Possum Trot's background noises were carefully considered by Weigel, who used them to establish a feeling of location and ambiance. Every sound, including the sounds of the natural world and neighborhood life, was included to enhance the film's realism and immersion.

Authenticity in Emotions:

Weigel's directing philosophy was centered on emotional candor. He intended for the movie to evoke strong feelings in viewers, urging them to identify with the characters and their journey. Weigel concentrated on capturing authentic emotional moments in his work, whether they were through close-knit character exchanges or stirring neighborhood scenes.

To give their performances a sense of reality, Weigel encouraged the actors to draw on their feelings and experiences. In several sequences, he also employed improvisation, which gave the actors more freedom to explore their roles and provide impromptu, genuine moments. This method contributed to making a movie that seemed authentic and immediate, perfectly encapsulating the essence of the Possum Trot tale.

Depth Thematic:

Weigel was dedicated to delving into the Possum Trot story's rich conceptual complexity. In addition to addressing significant social and cultural challenges, he wanted the movie to offer a resilient and hopeful message. The narrative was interwoven with themes of community, faith, and tenacity, resulting in a thought-provoking and inspirational movie.

Weigel made deliberate creative decisions regarding the narrative and visual aesthetic to emphasize these topics. He emphasized the themes with symbolism and visual metaphors, such as the representation of optimism and despair through light and dark. The inner struggles of the characters and their path toward optimism were also reflected in the dialogue.

"Sound of Hope: The Story of Possum Trot" was directed by Joshua Weigel, who was deeply committed to emotional storytelling, teamwork, and honesty. Weigel brought the inspirational true story of Possum Trot to life on screen using painstaking planning, imaginative decision-making, and a collaborative attitude. His focus on thematic depth, inventive narrative structure, and meticulous attention to detail produced a film that inspires viewers to consider the strength of community and optimism in addition to being highly entertaining.

Weigel's goal for "Sound of Hope" went beyond only making a movie; it also involved developing a narrative that would uplift and unite people. Weigel has produced a piece of art that honors the tenacity of the human spirit and the enduring force of hope by perfectly encapsulating the essence of the Possum Trot community and their journey.

CHAPTER 9

EDITING AND POST-PRODUCTION

Post-production Process: Editing, Sound Design, and Special Effects

Editing: Crafting the Narrative

Editing is the heartbeat of filmmaking, where raw footage is transformed into a coherent, compelling story. For "Sound of Hope: The Story of Possum Trot," the editing process was a meticulous journey, aimed at preserving the authenticity and emotional depth of the true events that inspired the film.

Initial Assembly

The post-production phase began with the initial assembly, where all the filmed scenes were arranged in the order they appeared in the script. This rough cut provided a broad overview of the narrative flow and helped identify areas that needed refinement. Joshua Weigel, the director, worked closely with the lead editor, Alex Thompson, to ensure that the initial assembly captured the essence of each scene.

Fine-Tuning the Story

Once the rough cut was completed, the process of fine-tuning began. This phase involved trimming unnecessary footage, tightening transitions, and ensuring that each scene flowed seamlessly into the next. The goal was to create a rhythm and pacing that would keep audiences engaged from start to finish. This often meant making difficult decisions, such as cutting scenes that, while beautifully shot, did not advance the story or develop the characters further.

Maintaining Emotional Continuity

One of the biggest challenges in editing "Sound of Hope" was maintaining the emotional continuity of the film. The story of Possum Trot is filled with poignant moments of struggle, resilience, and hope. Ensuring that these emotions resonated authentically required careful attention to performance nuances and timing. Weigel and Thompson spent countless hours reviewing takes, selecting the ones that best conveyed the intended emotions, and positioning them at precise moments to maximize their impact.

Sound Design: Enhancing the Atmosphere

Sound design plays a crucial role in immersing the audience in the world of the film. For "Sound of Hope," the sound design team, led by renowned sound designer, Sarah Bennett, focused on creating an auditory landscape that complemented the film's visual storytelling.

Dialogue Editing

Clear and crisp dialogue is essential for conveying the narrative and ensuring that audiences can follow the story. During the dialogue editing phase, Bennett's team meticulously cleaned up the audio tracks, removing any unwanted background noise, and ensuring that the actors' voices were consistently clear. This process often involved syncing ADR (Automated Dialogue Replacement) recordings with the original footage to replace lines that were inaudible or distorted during filming.

Creating Ambiance

The ambiance of Possum Trot, a small, close-knit community, was brought to life through detailed soundscapes. Bennett and her team recorded ambient sounds from similar rural environments, including bird calls, rustling leaves, and distant church bells. These sounds were layered into the film to create a rich auditory backdrop that enhanced the setting and mood of each scene.

Music and Score

Music is a powerful tool in evoking emotions and underscoring dramatic moments. Composer James Newton Howard was brought on board to create the film's score. Howard's music weaved through the narrative, accentuating moments of tension, sorrow, and triumph. The score was recorded with a live orchestra, adding a layer of depth and richness that elevated the film's emotional impact.

Special Effects: Augmenting Reality

While "Sound of Hope" is primarily a drama rooted in real events, special effects were used subtly to enhance the storytelling and create visual continuity.

Digital Enhancements

Digital enhancements were applied to ensure consistency in the visual tone of the film. Color grading was a significant aspect of this process, with the colorist working closely with Weigel to develop a color palette that reflected the film's themes. Warm, earthy tones were used to evoke a sense of community and tradition, while cooler hues highlighted moments of isolation and conflict.

Visual Effects Integration

In a few key scenes, visual effects were used to create elements that were impractical or impossible to film. For example, a storm scene required digital effects to convincingly portray the intensity of the weather while ensuring the safety of the cast and crew. These effects were seamlessly integrated into the live-action footage, maintaining a realistic look that did not distract from the story.

Balancing Artistic Vision with Technical Execution

Achieving a balance between artistic vision and technical execution is often a delicate process in filmmaking. For "Sound of Hope," this balance was crucial in ensuring that the film remained true to its source material while also delivering a polished and engaging cinematic experience.

Collaboration and Communication

Effective collaboration and communication between the director, editors, sound designers, and visual effects artists were essential. Regular meetings and review sessions allowed the team to align on the film's vision and address any technical challenges that arose. Joshua Weigel's ability to articulate his creative vision helped guide the technical team in executing their tasks while maintaining the film's artistic integrity.

Adapting to Constraints

Like any production, "Sound of Hope" faced its share of constraints, including budget limitations and time pressures. The post-production team had to find innovative solutions to deliver high-quality results within these constraints. For instance, the use of digital effects was carefully planned to ensure they added value without escalating costs. Similarly, the sound design team maximized their resources by using a combination of field recordings and sound libraries to create the film's auditory landscape.

Testing and Feedback

Throughout the post-production process, test screenings were conducted to gather feedback from select audiences. These screenings provided valuable insights into how the film was received and highlighted areas that needed improvement. Based on the feedback, the team made adjustments to the edit, sound design, and effects to enhance the overall viewing experience.

Final Touches

As the post-production phase neared completion, the focus shifted to polishing the final product. This involved fine-tuning the audio mix, ensuring the final cut was perfectly timed, and conducting a final color grade to unify the film's visual style. These final touches were crucial in ensuring that "Sound of Hope" met the high standards set by the filmmakers and resonated with audiences on both an emotional and aesthetic level.

"Sound of Hope" and the Impact of Post-Production.

"Sound of Hope: The Story of Possum Trot's editing and post-production procedures served as a tribute to the teamwork needed to make a movie come to life. With careful editing, creative sound design, and nuanced visual effects, the group was able to produce a video that not only tells a compelling tale but also fully immerses the viewer in the Possum Trot universe. The filmmakers made sure that the finished product accurately reflected the optimism and resiliency that served as the story's inspiration by striking a balance between technical execution and creative vision.

CHAPTER 10

SECURING DISTRIBUTION

The Deal with Angel Studios

The acquisition of distribution rights marked a significant turning point in the process of bringing "Sound of Hope: The Story of Possum Trot" to the big screen. The film's North American distribution rights were acquired by Angel Studios, a company well-known for its creative distribution tactics and previous box office successes, it was announced in February 2024. This collaboration was not just a business arrangement; rather, it was a calculated move to increase the movie's impact and audience.

Angel Studios recognized that "Sound of Hope" had the same ability to connect with viewers as

"Sound of Freedom," which had brought them significant attention and financial success in 2023. Their strong network of supporters and proficiency in community outreach and grassroots marketing made them the perfect distributor for "Sound of Hope."

Choosing to work with Angel Studios was motivated by some important considerations. Firstly, Angel Studios was no stranger to producing films with powerful social messages; in fact, this was a natural fit with the ideas of "Sound of Hope." The story of the movie, which was based on actual events and has as its main themes hope, community, and resilience, fit in perfectly with Angel Studios' goal of creating and releasing inspirational and uplifting media.

Second, "Sound of Freedom" commercial success and creative distribution tactics proved Angel

Studios could manage and market movies that weren't part of the established Hollywood circuit. Their strategy promised to give "Sound of Hope" a focused and successful marketing push. It frequently involved utilizing their sizable mailing list, social media presence, and direct connection with faith-based and value-driven audiences.

The agreement was made to guarantee that the success of the movie would benefit Angel Studios as well as the filmmakers. It had clauses that permitted an extensive promotional plan, a significant marketing expenditure, and a broad theatrical release. Additionally, the contract had provisions that guaranteed the filmmaker's creative authority over the film's distribution to the general public, preserving the film's moral integrity and message.

The Marketing Strategies

After the distribution agreement was signed, attention turned to marketing plans that would guarantee "Sound of Hope" was heard by the right people and beyond. The film's captivating tale and the positive publicity that resulted from Angel Studios' involvement served as the foundation for the marketing strategy.

Making Use of Past Achievements:

A primary tactic was to use the popularity of "Sound of Freedom." The marketing team realized that because "Sound of Hope" and "Sound of Freedom" shared a common theme of strong, factual stories, the audiences who backed "Sound of Freedom" were probably also likely to be interested in "Sound of Hope." The group wanted to establish a feeling of expectation and continuity by tying "Sound of Hope" into the story of achievement and societal influence that "Sound of Freedom" had fostered.

This was accomplished by utilizing focused promotion that emphasized the relationship between the two movies. Referencing the triumph of "Sound of Freedom," trailers and promotional materials frequently positioned "Sound of Hope" as the next inspirational tale from a reliable distributor. Potential viewers were already inclined to value the kind of storytelling that Angel Studios promoted, so this tactic helped foster a sense of enthusiasm and trust among them.

Grassroots marketing and community involvement:

The power of Angel Studios rested in their capacity to inspire community mobilization and grassroots movement-building around their films.

In the case of "Sound of Hope," this meant interacting with non-profits, churches, and community groups that shared the same values.

In collaboration with these organizations, screenings were arranged so they could hold unique events and debates about the movie. This strategy reached viewers for the movie who might not have been reached through conventional marketing means and gave community leaders and members a sense of ownership and investment.

Campaigns on social media were still another essential element of the grassroots approach. Angel Studios' vast social media network allowed the marketing team to produce interesting and shareable content. Regularly released behind-the-scenes videos, cast and crew interviews, and anecdotes from the actual events that served as the inspiration for the movie kept viewers interested and created suspense.

Celebrity and Influencer Endorsements:

Understanding that public opinion might be influenced by celebrities and influencers, the marketing team went out to people who had a large following and a track record of supporting socially conscious initiatives. This was one area in which Letitia Wright, the movie's executive producer, excelled. Her participation in the initiative gained credibility and attention right away.

To promote the movie, Wright and the other cast members took part in podcasts, social media campaigns, and interviews. Their first-hand recommendations and behind-the-scenes information brought the marketing initiatives to life and strengthened the bond with prospective viewers.

Advance Screenings and Verbal Recommendations:

Two weeks before the official release date, on June 19, 2024, a studio-sponsored preview screening was a crucial component of the marketing plan. This was a well-planned event meant to create excitement and goodwill. Influencers, local authorities, movie reviewers, and particular members of the public who have demonstrated resolute support for Angel Studios' prior endeavors were invited.

The goal of the advance showing was to create an experience as much as to present the movie. The film's topics were discussed, attendees had the chance to ask questions of the actors and staff, and they were given the chance to post their opinions on social media. Before the theatrical premiere, this event was essential in generating excitement and establishing momentum.

The Film's Title Changed

The movie's title was changed to "Sound of Hope," which was one of the most calculated choices in the marketing strategy. Titled "The Story of Possum Trot," it was changed to better fit Angel Studios' identity and capitalize on the popularity of "Sound of Freedom."

Rationale Behind the Title Change:

Several marketing factors affected the choice to rename the product. First off, the film's main theme of hope and resiliency was instantly communicated with the new title, "Sound of Hope." With its promise of an emotionally stirring encounter, the title was sure to draw in a wider readership.

Secondly, the marketing team wanted to establish a feeling of familiarity and continuity by emulating the "Sound of Freedom" title structure. It was anticipated that audiences who had reacted favorably to "Sound of Freedom" would immediately identify with "Sound of Hope," raising the possibility of their interest and participation.

Implementing the Title Change:

The movie's website, social media accounts, trailers, posters, and other promotional materials all needed to be updated to implement the new title. Careful planning went into this rebranding initiative to guarantee uniformity across all media and to minimize misunderstandings among prospective viewers.

The marketing team also created a storyline around the title change, outlining it as a component of a larger plan to emotionally engage viewers. Press releases, interviews, and social media posts were used to spread this story, which helped to present the title change as a wise and strategic decision.

Reception by the Audience:

The title change received a resoundingly positive reception. The film's emotional impact and ability to encapsulate its essence in a concise title were highly applauded for the new title. The pre-release buzz was tremendous due to the curiosity and excitement caused by the alignment with Angel Studios' past success.

The success of "Sound of Hope: The Story of Possum Trot" depended heavily on obtaining distribution and developing a successful marketing plan. The film's platform was supportive and strategically matched with its topics thanks to the cooperation with Angel Studios. Through the utilization of prior triumphs, active involvement in communities, influencer promotion, and a well-received title modification, the marketing team successfully generated a great deal of buzz and expectation for the movie's debut.

In addition to positioning "Sound of Hope" for financial success, the all-encompassing distribution and marketing strategy made sure that the film's message of hope, community, and resiliency was heard by a large and attentive audience. The foundation created by these initiatives promised to turn "Sound of Hope" into more than just a cinematic event, but also a cultural moment that would elevate and inspire audiences across North America as the film got ready for its July 4, 2024, theatrical debut.

CHAPTER 11

ADVANCED SCREENINGS AND INITIAL REACTIONS

As the studio-sponsored early showing of "Sound of Hope: The Story of Possum Trot" drew near, excitement for the film intensified. Angel Studios planned this event, which was set for June 19, 2024, as a calculated effort to generate excitement and get early input from a small number of attendees before the movie's July 4, 2024, national release. The advance screening served as more than just a sneak peek; it was a masterfully planned occasion meant to create excitement and lay the groundwork for the film's anticipated profitable run in theaters.

The Location and Ambience

The Fox Theatre in Atlanta, Georgia, a historic site selected for its grandeur and significance in the Southern United States, hosted the advance showing. The movie's title illuminated the theater's famous marquee and gave guests an eye-catching first impression. The site selection also emphasized the movie's ties to its Southern heritage, adding to the realism of the cinematic experience.

A red carpet welcomed attendees, and reporters and photographers were there to document the excitement. Film critics, business executives, local dignitaries, and fans who had won tickets through various promotional contests made up the gathering. The cast and crew of the movie, including Elizabeth Mitchell, Demetrius Grosse, Nika King, Joshua Weigel, Diaana Babnicova, and executive producer Letitia Wright were among the prominent guests.

There was a tangible sense of expectancy in the air, and the mood was electric. In the foyer, guests conversed about the film's significance and their expectations. A brief display presenting the true story of Possum Trot was also part of the event; it included pictures, newspaper articles, and artifacts that offered background information about the era.

The Screening Experience

The audience quieted as the lights went down and the screen flared to life. Director Joshua Weigel gave a brief introduction and dedicated the movie to the real-life Possum Trot community, stressing the significance of the narrative and the painstaking care that went into portraying it. The watching experience was made more respectful and sincere by this personal touch.

The film's compelling story and arresting images captured the audience's attention from the very first moments. The way Elizabeth Mitchell portrayed Susan Ramsey drew the audience in and captured the story's emotional essence. The genuine and emotional relationship between Demetrius Grosse and Nika King, who portrayed Donna Martin and Reverend Martin, respectively, enhanced the film's examination of community and resiliency.

The film's tempo and structure were thoughtfully designed to keep viewers interested, striking a balance between tense inspirational, and hopeful parts. The cinematography, which emphasized Georgia's gorgeous surroundings, gave the story a visually striking backdrop that improved the narrative. Renowned composer's music well matched the story, giving important moments a deeper emotional quality.

Initial Reactions from the Audience

The audience exploded in cheers as the credits rolled, a testament to the film's effect. The first responses were highly good, with many viewers applauding the movie for being real, having a deep emotional impact, and having excellent acting.

A local journalist's comment, "Sound of Hope is a triumph in storytelling," was one noteworthy response. It not only gracefully and sensitively illuminates a significant historical narrative, but it also does so. The directing is flawless, and the performances are outstanding."

Attending film critics were quick to post their opinions on social media, with several pointing out the movie's potential for nominations for prizes. Just finished watching an advance showing of #SoundOfHope," a well-known film reviewer tweeted. This movie is a masterwork of poignant narrative. Oscar-worthy performances are given by Demetrius Grosse and Elizabeth Mitchell. Take note of this one!"

Social media was another platform used by audience members to show their appreciation. A fan wrote on Instagram, saying, "Sound of Hope tonight was amazing. Possum Trot's narrative is masterfully narrated. I'm still considering it. Many people's hearts will be touched by this movie.

Important Preliminary Reviews

Early evaluations from well-known critics were also possible thanks to the advanced screening; several of them were keen to share their opinions.

These reviews were extremely important in influencing public opinion and creating buzz about the movie's upcoming broader distribution.

"Sound of Hope": The Story of Possum Trot is an evocative and poignant portrayal of community strength and the power of hope," stated one review in a reputable cinema magazine. The film's emotional highs and lows are expertly balanced by director Joshua Weigel, who crafts a narrative that is both inspiring and heartbreaking. Elizabeth Mitchell had an outstanding portrayal as Susan Ramsey, perfectly encapsulating the spirit of a compassionate and determined lady."

An influential online film platform also gave the film's production standards and plot high marks, writing, "Sound of Hope immerses viewers in the world of Possum Trot with its breathtaking cinematography and stirring score." Every aspect of the movie, from the intricate set designs to the subtle acting, demonstrates the film's commitment to authenticity. The way that Demetrius Grosse and Nika King portrayed the Martins is remarkable; they gave their characters a sincere feeling of warmth and resiliency."

The film's handling of delicate subjects and social relevance were other praises from critics. This feature was noted in a review published in a major newspaper: "Sound of Hope is more than just a movie; it's a potent meditation on the resilience of the human spirit in the face of hardship. It sensitively tackles problems of poverty, community, and faith in a way that is thought-provoking and inspirational. Anyone looking for a story that has a profound human resonance should watch this movie."

Early Reactions' Impact

The favorable responses and evaluations from the advance screening had an instant effect on the movie's future. Attendees' and reviewers' social media buzz spread, trending the hashtag #SoundOfHope across a range of channels. Potential viewers' interest was piqued by this online momentum, and many of them commented how excited they were to see the movie when it was officially released.

Angel Studios released more promotional materials, such as behind-the-scenes videos and cast and crew interviews, to take advantage of this surge of interest. These initiatives increased the movie's exposure and strengthened the idea that "Sound of Hope" was a significant work of art and society.

The directors received insightful input from the early viewing as well. Even though the reaction to the movie was overwhelmingly positive, some viewers had constructive comments to share about some parts of it. For instance, some viewers thought that to keep the momentum going, the second act's pacing could have been tighter. Joshua Weigel and his group took these observations to heart, making small tweaks here and there to make the final cut as powerful as possible.

June 19, 2024's previews showing of "Sound of Hope: The Story of Possum Trot" was a huge success, paving the way for the movie's general release. The occasion emphasized the film's social and emotional impact in addition to showcasing its artistic qualities. The picture had the potential to have a big impact on the box office and the cultural dialogue, based on the positive responses from the crowd and the early reviews from reviewers.

The anticipation created by the early screening of "Sound of Hope" intensified as the release date drew nearer, indicating a robust premiere and enduring impact. This point in the movie's narrative emphasizes how crucial planned early screenings are to influencing public opinion and laying the groundwork for future success. The enthusiastic response to the advance showing was evidence of the effort and commitment of all those involved in bringing Possum Trot's story to the big screen and making sure that its inspirational and resilient message found a receptive audience.

CHAPTER 12

THEATRICAL RELEASE ON JULY 4, 2024

Nationwide Release Strategy

The nationwide release of "Sound of Hope: The Story of Possum Trot" on July 4, 2024, was meticulously planned to ensure maximum reach and impact. This date was chosen for its symbolic significance—America's Independence Day—a day that represents freedom, hope, and the enduring spirit of resilience, perfectly aligning with the film's themes.

Marketing Campaign

The marketing campaign for the film was multi-faceted, utilizing both traditional and digital media to create buzz and anticipation. Angel Studios, known for its successful marketing strategies, played a crucial role in orchestrating the campaign.

Traditional Media:

Television and Radio Ads: Leading up to the release, high-frequency advertisements were aired on major networks and popular radio stations. These ads featured compelling snippets from the film, focusing on its emotional and inspirational aspects.

Print Media: Full-page ads and features in leading newspapers and magazines highlighted the film's unique story and its relevance. Interviews with the cast and crew, particularly with Letitia Wright, were published in high-profile publications, providing deeper insights into the film's making and its message.

Billboards and Posters: Strategic placement of billboards in high-traffic areas, including major highways and city centers, ensured maximum visibility. The striking visuals from the film's key scenes and its evocative tagline "A Story of Resilience and Hope" captured the attention of passersby.

Digital Media:

Social Media Campaign: The film's social media strategy was robust, leveraging platforms like Facebook, Instagram, Twitter, and TikTok. A dedicated team created engaging content, including behind-the-scenes footage, interviews, character spotlights, and interactive posts to engage the audience. Hashtags like #SoundOfHope and #PossumTrotStory trended in the weeks leading up to the release.

Influencer Partnerships: Collaborations with influencers and celebrities who resonated with the film's themes amplified its reach. These influencers shared personal stories of hope and resilience, drawing parallels with the film and encouraging their followers to watch it.

YouTube and Online Ads: Trailers and teaser clips were promoted heavily on YouTube, ensuring that the film reached a broad audience. Online ads on popular websites and streaming platforms also played a crucial role in targeting potential viewers.

Advance Screenings and Word of Mouth

A critical component of the release strategy was the studio-sponsored advance screening held on June 19, 2024. This event was designed to build momentum and generate word-of-mouth buzz.

Exclusive Screenings:

Media and Influencer Previews: Selected journalists, critics, and influencers were invited to exclusive screenings. This generated early reviews and social media buzz, setting a positive tone for the film's public release.

Community Screenings: Special screenings were held in various communities, particularly in areas that resonated with the film's story. These events were often accompanied by discussions and Q&A sessions with cast members and filmmakers, creating a deeper connection with the audience.

Positive Reviews and Testimonials:

Critical Acclaim: Early reviews praised the film's storytelling, performances, and its powerful message. Critics highlighted the authenticity of the narrative and the stellar performances of the cast, particularly Elizabeth Mitchell and Demetrius Grosse.

Audience Reactions: Attendees of the advance screenings took to social media to share their heartfelt reactions. Many spoke of being moved to tears and feeling inspired, which encouraged a wider audience to watch the film upon its release.

Box Office Performance

The box office performance of "Sound of Hope: The Story of Possum Trot" was a testament to the effective release strategy and the film's universal appeal. The film opened in 2,800 theaters across North America, with additional international releases planned in subsequent weeks.

Opening Weekend

Record-Breaking Numbers:

High Grossing Debut: The film debuted to impressive numbers, grossing $25 million in its opening weekend. This was a remarkable achievement for a drama film, underscoring its widespread appeal and the effectiveness of the marketing campaign.

Strong Per-Screen Average: The per-screen average was notably high, indicating strong audience interest and engagement. Many theaters reported sold-out shows, particularly during prime-time screenings.

Demographic Insights:

Diverse Audience: The film attracted a diverse audience, cutting across age, gender, and cultural backgrounds. While it resonated strongly with families and older viewers, its inspirational themes also drew younger audiences.

Geographical Spread: Urban centers saw higher turnout rates, but the film also performed well in suburban and rural areas, reflecting its broad appeal and relatable story.

Sustained Success

Positive Word of Mouth:

Social Media Influence: The positive reactions and reviews shared on social media continued to drive interest and attendance. Hashtags related to the film remained trending for several days post-release.

Community Endorsements: Various community leaders, educators, and activists endorsed the film, organizing group viewings and discussions, which sustained audience interest.

Repeat Viewership:

Emotional Impact: The film's powerful message led many viewers to watch it multiple times, often bringing friends and family along for subsequent viewings. This repeat viewership significantly boosted overall box office numbers.

Extended Runs: Due to high demand, many theaters extended the film's run beyond the initial release window. Some theaters even brought it back for special showings weeks after its debut.

International Performance:

Global Appeal: The film's themes of hope and resilience had universal appeal, leading to successful international releases. Countries with significant interest included the United Kingdom, Canada, Australia, and several European and Asian nations.

Festival Circuit: Before its wide international release, the film was showcased at several international film festivals, where it received critical acclaim and won multiple awards. This further bolstered its reputation and attracted global audiences.

Audience Engagement

The engagement of the audience was a critical factor in the film's success. The filmmakers and Angel Studios employed several strategies to ensure that the audience remained connected and invested in the film.

Interactive Experiences

Online Platforms:

Dedicated Website: A comprehensive website provides information about the film, including behind-the-scenes content, cast interviews, and a blog featuring stories related to the film's themes.

Virtual Screenings and Q&A Sessions: Virtual screenings followed by live Q&A sessions with the cast and crew allowed fans to engage directly with the filmmakers. These sessions were highly popular and often streamed on social media platforms.

Educational Initiatives:

School Partnerships: The film's educational value was leveraged through partnerships with schools and educational institutions. Study guides and discussion materials were provided to facilitate classroom discussions about the film's themes.

Community Programs: Collaborations with community organizations and faith-based groups facilitated screenings and discussions, furthering the film's reach and impact.

Merchandise and Memorabilia

Thematic Merchandise:

Branded Items: T-shirts, posters, and other merchandise featuring key quotes and imagery from the film were made available. These items were popular among fans and served as tangible reminders of the film's message.

Special Editions: Limited edition DVDs and Blu-rays, including bonus content such as director's commentary and deleted scenes, were released, catering to collectors and enthusiasts.

Charitable Collaborations:

Fundraising Efforts: Portions of the proceeds from merchandise sales were donated to charities and organizations that supported the themes of the film, such as foster care and community development programs. This initiative resonated with the audience and encouraged purchases.

Critical Acclaim and Awards

The critical acclaim and numerous awards that "Sound of Hope: The Story of Possum Trot" received played a significant role in sustaining its momentum.

Critical Reviews:

Top Critics' Praise: Renowned film critics lauded the film for its heartfelt narrative, strong performances, and its powerful social message. The performances of Elizabeth Mitchell and Demetrius Grosse were particularly highlighted.

Rotten Tomatoes and Metacritic Scores: The film maintained high ratings on review aggregator sites like Rotten Tomatoes and Metacritic, further validating its quality and appeal.

Awards and Recognitions:

Film Festivals: The film was showcased at several prestigious film festivals, winning awards for Best Picture, Best Director, and Best Actor/Actress.

Industry Awards: It received nominations and awards from major industry bodies, including the Golden Globes and the Academy Awards, enhancing its credibility and attracting a broader audience.

Impact and Legacy

The impact and legacy of "Sound of Hope: The Story of Possum Trot" extend beyond its box office success. The film has inspired social change and sparked important conversations about resilience, community, and the power of hope.

Social Impact:

Community Outreach: Inspired by the film, various community outreach programs were initiated, focusing on education, foster care, and support for underprivileged communities.

Advocacy and Awareness: The film brought attention to the issues faced by communities like Possum Trot, leading to increased advocacy and support for relevant causes.

Inspirational Legacy:

Cultural Phenomenon: The film became a cultural touchstone, inspiring other filmmakers and storytellers to explore similar themes and stories of resilience.

Personal Stories: Many individuals shared personal stories of how the film impacted their lives, reinforcing the film's message of hope and the human spirit's capacity to overcome adversity.

The theatrical release of "Sound of Hope: The Story of Possum Trot" on July 4, 2024, was a carefully orchestrated event that successfully combined strategic marketing, critical acclaim, and audience engagement. The film's impressive box office performance and its enduring impact are testaments to the power of storytelling and the universal appeal of themes that resonate deeply with the human experience. Through its portrayal of resilience and hope, "Sound of Hope: The Story of Possum Trot" has left an indelible mark on audiences worldwide, continuing to inspire and uplift.

CHAPTER 13

CRITICAL AND PUBLIC RECEPTION

Comprehensive Reviews from Critics

Critics have responded to "Sound of Hope: The Story of Possum Trot" in a variety of ways, with many praising its performances, emotional depth, and storytelling. The film's critical reception can be divided into many thematic evaluations, such as the film's technical execution, director's vision, acting intensity, and story authenticity.

Storytelling and Authenticity in Narrative

The narrative accuracy of the movie is one of its best-loved features. The screenplay by the Weigels expertly conveys the core of the actual events that served as the inspiration for the movie, according to critics. John DeFore, writing for The Hollywood Reporter, praised the movie for its "heartfelt portrayal of a community's struggle and triumph," emphasizing how the narrative doesn't sugarcoat the difficult truths that the residents of Possum Trot must deal with. Reviews frequently highlight the film's ability to strike a balance between hope and misery, with many critics praising its ability to tell an inspiring story without bordering on sentimentality.

Variety's Peter Debruge emphasized how well the screenplay creates multifaceted characters that capture the complexity of the real-life equivalents. He said, "The Weigels' script doesn't just tell a story; it breathes life into its characters, making their journey compelling and relatable." The popularity of the movie has been attributed in large part to this subtle storytelling, which immerses audiences in Possum Trot's environment and increases their stake in the resolution.

Performances

The "Sound of Hope" cast members have received a great deal of praise. The nuance and realism of Elizabeth Mitchell's portrayal of Susan Ramsey have drawn particular attention. According to Manohla Dargis's review in The New York Times, Mitchell's portrayal was "a masterclass in subtlety and strength," perfectly encapsulating the emotional fortitude of a woman driven to make a difference. One of the main factors contributing to the film's emotional effect has been identified as Mitchell's capacity to portray a variety of emotions, from quiet resolve to deep grief.

The way Demetrius Grosse played Reverend Martin has also received a lot of praise. The Los Angeles Times' Justin Chang observed, "Grosse brings a gravitas and warmth to the role that anchors the film's moral and emotional core." His depiction of a devout man struggling to balance his obligations to his family and community gives the story additional depth and enhances audience resonance.

Both Joshua Weigel's portrayal of Pastor Mark and Nika King's portrayal of Donna Martin have received praise for their emotional depth and realism. Particular attention has been paid to King's portrayal of a woman who faces both personal and societal issues with dignity and resolve. Along with directing, Weigel contributes a subtle performance that enhances the group cast, resulting in a convincing and well-rounded portrait of the Possum Trot neighborhood.

Vision for Directing

Another subject of criticism has been Joshua Weigel's direction style. His skill in balancing the film's many parts to create a cogent and emotionally compelling narrative has been commended by critics. According to David Ehrlich of IndieWire, "Weigel's direction is both sensitive and assured, allowing the story to unfold naturally while maintaining a strong emotional undercurrent."

One important aspect of the film's authenticity has been attributed to Weigel's decision to film in Macon, Georgia. The story is set against a rich backdrop of natural beauty and historical significance, which heightens the story's emotional appeal. Weigel's cooperation with the neighborhood during filming has also been praised as a good element that gave the movie more layers of realism and involvement.

Technical Performance

Technically speaking, "Sound of Hope" has received accolades for its score, sound design, and cinematography. The unadulterated beauty of the Georgian terrain is captured by David Lanzenberg's cinematography, which contrasts the natural setting with the internal human turmoil. According to critics, the film's strong feeling of place and visual aesthetic heighten its emotional impact.

Both the soundtrack and the sound design have gotten positive reviews. Film Score Monthly called composer John Paesano's score "hauntingly beautiful," noting how the orchestral and folk elements he used to enhance the film's themes created an emotional undercurrent. The film's immersive effect is enhanced by the sound design, which makes the audience feel as though they are a member of the Possum Trot community, especially in scenes that show church services and community events.

Public Reception and Impact on Viewers

Beyond the praise of critics, "Sound of Hope" has struck a profound chord with the general population, stirring powerful feelings and igniting conversations about social justice, community, and perseverance. Advance screenings and the theatrical release of the film have given us a chance to observe audience reactions and comprehend the story's wider significance.

Emotional Cooperation

The film has been praised for its capacity to arouse strong emotions in the public. People in the audience have often reported being brought to tears by the story's portrayal of adversity and hope. Viewers have been posting a lot of their emotional responses on social media, especially on Twitter and Instagram. These posts frequently include hashtags like #SoundOfHope and #PossumTrot. Many viewers have expressed admiration for the real-life folks who served as inspiration for the film, revealing a shared sense of connection to the characters and their journey through these posts.

Conversations in the Community and Their Social Impact

Additionally, the movie has spurred conversations in the community regarding the issues it tackles.

Numerous viewers have expressed how "Sound of Hope" inspired them to think about their communities and methods to help and encourage people in need. Community centers, churches, and educational institutions across the nation have arranged film-inspired talks and events, providing forums for individuals to convene and deliberate on topics related to poverty, resiliency, and collaborative efforts.

The reaction from different church groups, who have used the movie as a catalyst for conversations about faith and social justice, is one noteworthy example. These organizations have commended the movie for its genuine depiction of a community motivated by compassion and faith, which has encouraged them to think about how they may improve their communities. The way the church is portrayed in the Possum Trot community in the movie has struck an especially deep chord with viewers, underscoring the ability of religiously motivated projects to promote constructive change.

Impact on Education

Teachers have also acknowledged the movie's potential as an instructional resource. Incorporating "Sound of Hope" into their curricula, educators in high school and college use it to address issues like social justice, community development, and the strength of grassroots movements. The film's in-depth depiction of the difficulties the Possum Trot community faces serves as a useful case study for students, encouraging conversations on how theoretical ideas are applied in practical settings.

The movie has been shown in some educational seminars and workshops in addition to formal educational settings. With guest speakers including social professionals, community activists, and even residents of Possum Trot, these events have given attendees the chance to delve deeper into the topics of the movie. The discourse has enhanced the spectators' comprehension of the film's background and its wider societal ramifications.

Long-Term Impact and Legacy

Though the full effects of "Sound of Hope" are still being felt, preliminary evidence points to the movie's potential to make a significant impact down the road. More recognition and assistance for the actual Possum Trot community are among the most important effects of this influence. Some nonprofits saw an increase in donations and volunteer requests after the movie's premiere, attributed to viewers who were motivated to become involved.

The movie has also inspired other filmmakers and storytellers to investigate comparable tales, underscoring the significance of sharing tales of hope and resiliency in underprivileged areas. This trend may broaden the range of stories that are told in the media, which could foster empathy and understanding between various societal groups.

Viewer Remarks

Viewers' testimonies shed additional light on the movie's influence. Numerous people have mentioned how the movie encouraged them to become active in their neighborhoods, whether it was by giving money, volunteering, or just being kind to their neighbors. An Atlanta-based watcher, for example, posted on Facebook, saying, "Watching 'Sound of Hope' made me realize how much power we as individuals have to make a difference." I recently began helping at a nearby shelter, and I can't say enough how fulfilling it is."

A New York college student who was among the viewers shared on Instagram, saying, "This movie has altered my understanding of what it means to be a part of a community." Possum Trot's tale demonstrates how seemingly insignificant deeds may have a profound effect. I'm motivated to launch a university-wide community service organization."

These testimonies highlight the movie's capacity to motivate viewers to take specific action and develop a sense of accountability and empowerment.

Public and Critical Synergy

The way the audience and critics have reacted to the movie together has been a major factor in increasing its influence. Reputable critics' positive reviews have verified the film's artistic and thematic characteristics, resulting in a greater number of people seeing it. The positive reception from the general people has strengthened the positive reviews from critics, generating a positive feedback loop that has increased the film's exposure and impact.

The public's and critics' discussions have enhanced the discourse surrounding the movie as a whole. Viewers now have a better awareness and comprehension of the film's themes and technical aspects thanks to critics' evaluations. The public's emotional and subjective responses, meantime, have brought attention to the movie's social effect potential and applicability to real life, expanding the critical conversation.

Challenges and Criticisms

"Sound of Hope" has received a lot of favorable feedback, yet it has also drawn some criticism. Some critics have noted that the movie occasionally uses clichés and that some of the story's elements could have been developed further. For example, some have claimed that the movie should have given more background information regarding the structural problems that the Possum Trot community is facing.

A small percentage of viewers have also voiced dissatisfaction with the movie's pacing, claiming that some sequences were too dramatic or drawn out. Nevertheless, the film's numerous positive aspects and the strong emotional reaction it has generated have usually eclipsed these criticisms.

"Sound of Hope: The Story of Possum Trot" has received a great deal of praise from both the public and reviewers, and it has struck a deep chord with both. Its genuine narrative, captivating acting, and outstanding directing have cemented its status as a notable 2024 picture. Beyond just being a work of art, the movie has encouraged audiences to get involved in their communities and think about how they may contribute to positive change.

The positive reception that "Sound of Hope" has received from the general public as well as the critical community indicates that the movie will have a long-lasting effect on both the film industry and society at large. The history of the Possum Trot community, now captured in the film, will surely inspire hope and action for years to come, just as the town itself continues to thrive and inspire.

CHAPTER 14

THE IMPACT OF SOUND OF HOPE

Reflection on the Film's Cultural and Social Impact

"Sound of Hope: The Story of Possum Trot" is more than just a film; it is a cultural touchstone that encapsulates the enduring spirit of a community and the transformative power of collective action. As the film navigates the complexities of the human experience, it offers a narrative that resonates deeply with audiences, sparking conversations about resilience, faith, and the unyielding quest for justice and community solidarity.

A Beacon of Inspiration

The inspirational power of "Sound of Hope" is among its most significant effects. The way the movie depicts the Possum Trot community's tenacity in the face of overwhelming adversity gives viewers everywhere hope. The film encourages viewers to believe in the possibility of change despite their obstacles by showcasing the true stories of people who refused to give up. Not only is this inspiration just sentimental; it frequently inspires viewers to take action by encouraging them to volunteer, donate, or support organizations that align with their values.

Cultural Resonance and Identity

The film's cultural impact is multifaceted. For one, it contributes significantly to the representation of African American communities in media. By showcasing the lives and struggles of the Possum

Trot residents, the film provides a counter-narrative to the often negative or stereotypical portrayals of Black communities. It emphasizes their strength, unity, and the profound sense of kinship that binds them. This representation is crucial in fostering a more inclusive and accurate depiction of diverse cultures and experiences in mainstream media.

Moreover, "Sound of Hope" delves into the theme of community identity, exploring how shared experiences and collective efforts shape and define a community. This exploration encourages viewers to reflect on their communities and the values that underpin them. The film's success in depicting these themes underscores the importance of storytelling that honors and accurately represents the intricacies of cultural identities.

Educational Value

The impact of "Sound of Hope" is also significantly influenced by its educational value. With its gripping story that can be used to highlight a variety of crucial subjects, from social justice and community organizing to faith and resilience, the movie is an effective tool for educators and advocates. The movie can serve as a springboard for talks, workshops, and initiatives at colleges, institutions, and community organizations that want to promote a deeper comprehension of these concerns.

In addition, the film's thorough portrayal of Possum Trot's social and historical background provides a wealth of information for anybody looking to learn more about the larger effects of systematic inequity and how communities may fight it. Through the incorporation of a true tale,

"Sound of Hope" elevates these conversations and increases audience accessibility and engagement.

Catalyst for Social Change

Perhaps the most significant impact of "Sound of Hope" is its potential to catalyze social change. The film does not shy away from depicting the harsh realities faced by the Possum Trot community, from poverty and systemic neglect to the personal and collective struggles of its residents. By bringing these issues to the forefront, the film raises awareness and prompts viewers to consider their role in addressing similar challenges in their communities.

The story of Possum Trot illustrates the power of grassroots movements and the importance of community-driven solutions. This narrative can inspire other communities to organize and advocate for themselves, demonstrating that change is possible even in the face of significant obstacles. The film's impact is thus not limited to its immediate audience; it extends to the broader societal discourse on social justice and community empowerment.

Encouraging Empathy and Understanding

"Sound of Hope" not only encourages viewers to take action but also develops empathy and compassion in them. The movie promotes a stronger emotional bond with the experiences of the Possum Trot people by fully engrossing viewers in their lives. As viewers learn to perceive the humanity in persons who are frequently excluded or disregarded, this connection can aid in the removal of barriers and a decrease in prejudice.

The movie's capacity to arouse empathy is especially significant given the divisive social atmosphere of today. "Sound of Hope" advances a more sympathetic and nuanced comprehension of other groups and their challenges, so aiding in the larger objective of cultivating increased social cohesiveness and reciprocity.

The Future of Storytelling Inspired by Real-Life Events

Evolving Narrative Techniques

The success of "Sound of Hope" points to a growing trend in the film industry towards storytelling that is rooted in real-life events. This approach offers a unique opportunity to engage audiences with narratives that are both compelling and grounded in reality. As filmmakers continue to explore this genre, we can expect to see the development of new narrative techniques that enhance the authenticity and emotional impact of these stories.

One such technique is the use of immersive storytelling, which seeks to draw viewers into the world of the characters in a more visceral way. This can involve the use of advanced cinematography, sound design, and even virtual reality technologies to create a more immersive viewing experience. By making the audience feel as though they are part of the story, filmmakers can create a deeper emotional connection and a more profound impact.

Emphasis on Diverse Voices

Diverse voices and opinions will probably be given more weight in storytelling in the future. Movies such as "Sound of Hope" exemplify the potency of narratives that mirror the realities of underrepresented groups and elevate their perspectives. This tendency is crucial for promoting more representation in the media as well as for adding a broader variety of tales and points of view to the cultural environment.

A wider variety of storylines that question accepted wisdom and provide fresh perspectives on the human condition should become more prevalent as more filmmakers from various backgrounds are allowed to share their stories. This variety in storytelling will support the development of a more accepting and compassionate society that values and celebrates the diversity of cultures and viewpoints.

Integration of Social Media and Interactive Platforms

The future of storytelling in the digital age will surely be shaped by the incorporation of interactive platforms and social media. These tools give viewers new possibilities to interact with stories and take part in the telling process. Filmmakers, for instance, can use social media to promote their films, provide behind-the-scenes photos, and communicate with fans in real-time.

Through more meaningful audience engagement, interactive tools like online forums and virtual events can also improve the storytelling experience. In addition to sharing their own stories and joining in on debates, viewers can even have an impact on the course of upcoming initiatives. This degree of involvement can increase the story's emotional effect and cultivate a more devoted and committed audience.

Collaborative Storytelling

Collaborative storytelling is another new trend, in which several voices are combined to produce a story that is richer and more nuanced. This strategy can be used in a variety of ways, such as having community members participate in the filmmaking process or co-writing scripts. It is possible to guarantee that various viewpoints are addressed and that the finished work is more inclusive and authentic by using collaborative storytelling.

"Sound of Hope" is a perfect illustration of how teamwork can improve a project. To ensure that the voices and experiences of the Possum Trot community were appropriately portrayed, the film's production team worked closely with them. This method not only gives the story more depth but also makes the people involved feel proud and like they have something to contribute.

Focus on Impact and Social Responsibility

The need for tales that have a significant impact and promote positive change is rising as viewers become more socially aware. Filmmakers are becoming more aware of their social effects and the power to motivate people to take action and become more conscious of their surroundings. The future of storytelling will probably be shaped by this sense of social responsibility, as more initiatives that try to change the world and focus on significant social concerns will certainly emerge.

"Sound of Hope" is a prime example of this movement since it uses its platform to draw attention to the challenges and victories faced by the Possum Trot community and to inspire others to support similar causes. The movie has an influence that goes beyond simple enjoyment; it sparks debate, informs viewers, and encourages social action.

The moving "Sound of Hope: The Story of Possum Trot" demonstrates the influence that narrative may have on people and society at large. Its ability to inspire, inform, and organize audiences is a clear indication of its cultural and social value. By emphasizing the tenacity and unity of the Possum Trot community, the movie provides a moving reminder of the strength of group effort and the enduring human spirit.

In terms of the future, "Sound of Hope's" popularity indicates a larger trend in the film business toward honest, varied, and socially significant real-life storytelling. The power of storytelling to promote empathy and effect change will only increase as long as filmmakers keep experimenting with novel narrative devices and provide a voice to underrepresented groups.

Filmmakers have more opportunities than ever to engage audiences and promote social change in a time when social media and interactive platforms are changing how we interact with stories. The film industry can maintain its critical role in creating a world that is more compassionate and just by embracing these tools and emphasizing inclusive, impactful storytelling.

"Sound of Hope" establishes a standard for the kind of narrative that will shape the future in addition to honoring the victories of a community. It is an appeal for both moviegoers and filmmakers to acknowledge the ability of storytelling to shed light on the human condition and to arouse hope and change in the world. The teachings from Possum Trot will ring true in the future, serving as a constant reminder of the enormous influence that a single narrative can have on the globe.

CHAPTER 15

CONTINUING THE LEGACY

Ongoing Initiatives Inspired by the Film

More than just providing entertainment, the publication of "Sound of Hope: The Story of Possum Trot" has spurred a flurry of efforts aimed at building community resilience, support, and transformation. Several ongoing projects and organizations have been inspired by the film's compelling message, which has found resonance with audiences worldwide in its representation of the hardships and successes faced by the Possum Trot community.

Programs for Community Development

The creation of community development initiatives based on the initiatives seen in Possum Trot has been one of the movie's most notable effects. Several nonprofits and philanthropic institutions have spearheaded the creation of programs centered on economic growth, healthcare, and education in marginalized areas.

Education Initiatives: Several groups have started after-school programs and scholarship funds to help the education of children in underprivileged communities, motivated by the commitment of Elizabeth Mitchell's character Susan Ramsey. These initiatives seek to give students the tools and direction they require for success by offering mentorship, life skills training, and academic help in addition to these other services.

Healthcare Access: Medical outreach initiatives have been formed in recognition of the necessity of healthcare, as exemplified by the hardships experienced by the Possum Trot community. In isolated and rural locations, mobile clinics and health camps are currently operational, providing free medical examinations, immunizations, and health education. These programs seek to close the gap in underserved people's access to healthcare and enhance their general well-being.

Outreach Based on Faith

The way that Pastor Mark and Reverend Martin are portrayed in the movie emphasizes how important faith-based leadership is to community support. Many religious institutions have stepped up their outreach programs in response to their inspirational lives, emphasizing the provision of both material and spiritual assistance to those in need.

Church-Sponsored Programs: All over the nation, churches have started food banks, clothes drives, and shelter supplies. In addition, they provide support groups and counseling services to people dealing with mental health concerns, addiction, and domestic abuse. The goal of these faith-based programs is to empower people in their communities by establishing a network of support.

Interfaith Collaborations: Various religious groups have joined forces to work toward shared objectives, motivated by the harmony and cooperation depicted in the movie. The goal of these interfaith partnerships is to alleviate societal concerns including hunger, homelessness, and educational inequality. Through combining their resources and efforts, these groups show the effectiveness of solidarity and group endeavor.

Advocating for Adoption and Foster Care

The way adoption and foster care are portrayed in "Sound of Hope" is among its most endearing features. Many people have been motivated to think about adoption and foster care by the characters' dedication to finding loving homes for underprivileged kids.

Adoption Awareness Campaigns: To increase public awareness of the need for foster and adoptive families, some organizations have started campaigns. These initiatives seek to debunk misconceptions regarding the adoption procedure and offer details on how individuals and families can become involved. These programs urge more individuals to open their hearts and homes by showcasing the positive effects on children's lives and sharing tales of successful adoptions.

Foster Families Support Networks: In response to the difficulties that foster families encounter, support networks have been set up to offer information, guidance, and emotional support. By providing training, support groups, and respite care, these networks make sure foster parents have the resources necessary to give the kids in their care stable, loving surroundings.

How the Story of the Possum Trot Still Encourages Hope and Change

The Possum Trot story, as told in "Sound of Hope," never ceases to uplift people's spirits and spur social change. Talks about social fairness, community solidarity, and the strength of perseverance have been sparked by the movie.

Motivating Individual Deeds of Goodwill

"Sound of Hope" is essentially a narrative on the ability of individual deeds to change the world. Numerous people have been motivated to perform deeds of kindness and service in their communities by the movie.

Volunteering and community service: Many people have been inspired to donate their time and skills by the selflessness of characters like Reverend Martin and Susan Ramsey. Serving soup meals, tutoring kids, or organizing neighborhood clean-up days are examples of selfless deeds that help to create stronger, more unified communities.

Random Acts of Kindness: A movement of random acts of kindness has also been generated by the film's message. Individuals are discovering tiny ways to make other people's days better, such as buying a stranger's coffee or writing uplifting messages in public areas. Even tiny actions like these have a positive ripple effect and serve as a reminder to people of the influence they have on other people.

Promoting Advocacy and Civic Engagement

Additionally, the movie has inspired viewers to take a more active role in social and civic issues. People have been inspired to take a position for the causes they support by "Sound of Hope" because it emphasizes the value of advocacy and group action.

Grassroots Movements: To address a range of societal challenges, grassroots movements have arisen, inspired by the community organizing initiatives portrayed in the movie. The main goals of these movements are to encourage community people to take action, advocate for changes to policies, and raise awareness. These efforts are centered on problems including access to healthcare, affordable housing, and educational reform.

Political Engagement: People are becoming more interested in local government and activism as a result of the movie, which has also encouraged greater political engagement. Watchers are making efforts to guarantee their voices are heard and their communities are represented by taking part in voter registration drives and town hall meetings.

Promoting a Culture of Adaptability

The emphasis on resilience is among the Possum Trot story's most enduring legacies. The movie shows how a community can pull together to overcome hardship, and viewers have found great resonance with this message.

Mental Health Awareness: Talks on mental health have been more prevalent as a result of the representation of individuals who face and overcome major obstacles. The goal of initiatives centered on mental health support and awareness is to lessen stigma and offer resources to people who are experiencing mental health problems. These initiatives have gained traction.

Resilience Training Programs: Individuals and communities have been the focus of resilience training programs created in response to the film. These courses concentrate on developing coping mechanisms, cultivating optimism, and establishing networks of support. These initiatives assist people and communities in overcoming obstacles and emerging stronger by teaching resilience.

Strengthening Community ties

"Sound of Hope" has emphasized the value of community and the power that results from cooperation. Attempts to create communities that are more cohesive and stronger have been sparked by this concept.

Community Activities and Gatherings: Towns and neighborhoods have planned activities that unite people, drawing inspiration from the spirit of community portrayed in the movie. These get-togethers, which range from town hall meetings and cultural festivals to block parties and potlucks, promote a feeling of community and togetherness.

Peer Support Networks: Because of the movie's emphasis on helping one another, peer support networks have been established. These networks give people a place to talk to each other about their experiences, give counsel, and offer emotional support. These networks fortify the community through various means, such as parenting groups, addiction rehabilitation sessions, or support circles for disenfranchised populations.

The Broader Cultural Impact

Beyond private and public projects, "Sound of Hope: The Story of Possum Trot" has impacted societal conversations about social justice, storytelling, and representation in the media.

Media Representation

The movie has helped to fuel the growing call for genuine, varied representation in the media. The filmmakers have emphasized the value of sharing underrepresented perspectives and experiences by narrating Possum Trot's story.

Diverse Storytelling: The popularity of "Sound of Hope" has inspired producers and directors to look for and present tales from a variety of viewpoints. As a result, there are now more movies and TV series that examine the experiences and lifestyles of underrepresented groups, encouraging viewers to have a deeper sense of empathy and comprehension.

Empowering Marginalized Voices: People from various communities have been motivated to pursue professions in the arts by the film's depiction of strong, resilient protagonists from underrepresented backgrounds. Aspiring authors, filmmakers, and actors are inspired to tell their own stories and add to the cultural narrative when they witness representations of themselves in the media.

Fairness in Society Lobbying

"Sound of Hope" is now a standard conversation topic for fairness and social justice. The film's examination of systemic issues and locally driven solutions has spurred significant discussions and advocacy initiatives.

Programs for Education: Teachers have included the movie in their lesson plans to teach pupils about resilience, social justice, and community activism. Students are encouraged to think critically about how they might contribute to good change and get a deeper grasp of the social concerns portrayed in the film by critically assessing the themes and characters.

Advocacy Campaigns: To increase awareness and rally support for their issues, social justice organizations have utilized the movie as a tactic. Discussions, conferences, and workshops centered on topics like racial justice, poverty reduction, and community empowerment frequently follow "Sound of Hope" screenings.

Conclusion

"Sound of Hope: The Story of Possum Trot" is more than a film; it is a movement. Its legacy continues to inspire individuals and communities to take action, support one another, and strive for a better future. Through ongoing initiatives and the continued resonance of its message, the story of Possum Trot serves as a beacon of hope and a testament to the power of resilience, kindness, and collective action.

The influence of "Sound of Hope" will surely only increase in the future, encouraging new generations to continue Possum Trot's legacy. Through the adoption of compassion, solidarity, and persistence as core principles, we can fortify our communities and establish a fairer and more equal society for everybody.

APPENDICES

Appendix A: Biographies of Key Figures (both real and from the film)

Reverend Martin (Real Life)

Reverend Martin, a pivotal figure in the Possum Trot community, is renowned for his tireless efforts to uplift and unify the town. Born and raised in a small town similar to Possum Trot, he understood the struggles and aspirations of his community intimately. His journey from a young, impassioned preacher to a revered community leader is marked by his relentless advocacy for education, social justice, and economic empowerment. His initiatives have included founding local support groups, organizing community outreach programs, and championing the construction of essential infrastructure.

Susan Ramsey (Real Life)

Susan Ramsey is a community organizer and social worker who has dedicated her life to the betterment of Possum Trot. With a background in social work and community planning, Susan moved to Possum Trot to spearhead a series of community development projects. Her compassionate approach and strategic thinking have led to the successful implementation of numerous programs aimed at improving the quality of life for residents. Her efforts in health care, education, and housing have left an indelible mark on the community.

Elizabeth Mitchell (Actress)

Elizabeth Mitchell is an acclaimed actress known for her versatile roles in film and television. With a career spanning over two decades, she has captivated audiences with her performances in

"Lost," "The Santa Clause," and "Revolution." In "Sound of Hope: The Story of Possum Trot," Elizabeth brings depth and empathy to the character of Susan Ramsey. Her dedication to accurately portraying real-life heroes shines through in her meticulous preparation and heartfelt performance.

Demetrius Grosse (Actor)

Demetrius Grosse is a talented actor recognized for his compelling roles in both film and television. His performances in "Justified," "Fear the Walking Dead," and "Lovecraft Country" have earned him critical acclaim. In this film, Demetrius takes on the role of Reverend Martin, embodying the character's charisma, leadership, and unwavering commitment to his community. His portrayal captures the essence of a man driven by faith and a deep sense of duty.

Nika King (Actress)

Nika King is an accomplished actress and comedian best known for her role in HBO's "Euphoria." With a background in stand-up comedy and theater, Nika brings a unique blend of humor and gravitas to her roles. In "Sound of Hope: The Story of Possum Trot," she plays Donna Martin, the supportive and strong-willed wife of Reverend Martin. Nika's performance highlights the resilience and determination of women who stand beside their partners in the fight for social justice.

Joshua Weigel (Actor/Director)

Joshua Weigel is a multifaceted artist, known for his work as an actor, director, and writer. He has directed several acclaimed short films and features, often focusing on themes of redemption and hope. In addition to directing "Sound of Hope:

The Story of Possum Trot," Joshua also steps in front of the camera as Pastor Mark. His dual role in the project underscores his deep personal connection to the story and his commitment to bringing it to life authentically.

Diaana Babnicova (Actress)

Diaana Babnicova is a young and promising actress whose talent has already garnered attention in the industry. In this film, she plays Terri, a central character whose journey reflects the challenges and triumphs of the youth in Possum Trot. Diaana's nuanced performance captures the innocence, struggles, and hope of a generation striving for a better future.

Appendix B: Timeline of Events

Early 2000s: The Genesis of Community Efforts

Reverend Martin and Susan Ramsey begin their grassroots initiatives in Possum Trot, focusing on education, health care, and economic empowerment.

2010: Major Community Milestones

Establishment of the Possum Trot Community Center, offering various social services and educational programs.

Launch of a community-driven health care initiative, providing free medical check-ups and health education.

2015: Turning Points

Reverend Martin's inspirational sermon galvanizes the community to take collective action.

Susan Ramsey secures a major grant for the development of affordable housing projects in Possum Trot.

2018: The Story Gains Attention

National media coverage of Possum Trot's remarkable turnaround.

Interest from filmmakers Joshua and Rebekah Weigel led to the initial concept for "Sound of Hope: The Story of Possum Trot."

2021: Pre-Production Phase

Completion of the screenplay by Joshua and Rebekah Weigel.

Casting announcements and preliminary location scouting in Macon, Georgia.

Fall 2022: Filming Begins

Principal photography takes place in Macon, Georgia.

Behind-the-scenes challenges and triumphs during the filming process.

February 2024: Distribution Deal

Angel Studios acquires North American distribution rights.

Strategic rebranding of the film to "Sound of Hope" to leverage the success of "Sound of Freedom."

June 19, 2024: Advance Screening

Studio-sponsored advance screening, generating early buzz and critical feedback.

July 4, 2024: Theatrical Release

Nationwide release of the film.

Initial box office performance and audience reactions.

Appendix C: Interviews with Cast and Crew

Interview with Elizabeth Mitchell

Q: What drew you to the role of Susan Ramsey?

A: Susan's story is incredibly inspiring. Her dedication to her community and her unwavering hope resonated deeply with me. I wanted to honor her legacy by bringing authenticity and emotion to the role.

Q: How did you prepare for the role?

A: I spent time in communities similar to Possum Trot, speaking with social workers and community organizers. Understanding their challenges and triumphs was crucial to portraying Susan accurately.

Interview with Demetrius Grosse

Q: What was the most challenging aspect of playing Reverend Martin?

A: Capturing the depth of his faith and his commitment to his community was challenging. I wanted to ensure that I conveyed his strength and compassion in a way that felt genuine and impactful.

Q: Can you share a memorable moment from the set?

A: One of the most memorable moments was filming a sermon scene. The energy and emotion in the room were palpable, and it felt like we were truly honoring Reverend Martin's spirit.

Interview with Joshua Weigel

Q: What inspired you to direct this film?

A: The story of Possum Trot is a powerful testament to the strength of community and the human spirit. I was inspired by the real-life heroes and their unwavering hope, and I wanted to bring their stories to a wider audience.

Q: How did you balance your roles as director and actor?

A: It was a challenge, but having a great team made it possible. I trusted my crew to handle the technical aspects while I focused on my performance and directing the cast.

Interview with Rebekah Weigel (Co-Writer)

Q: What was the writing process like for this film?

A: It was a collaborative effort that involved a lot of research and interviews with real-life figures. We wanted to ensure that the screenplay was not only engaging but also true to the spirit of Possum Trot's story.

Q: What message do you hope audiences take away from the film?

A: We hope audiences are inspired by the power of hope and community. The film is a reminder that even in the face of adversity, collective action and unwavering faith can lead to transformative change.

Interview with Nika King

Q: How did you connect with your character, Donna Martin?

A: Donna's strength and resilience were qualities I deeply admired. I drew from my own experiences and the stories of women who have stood strong in the face of challenges to bring authenticity to their characters.

Q: What was the atmosphere like on set?

A: The atmosphere was incredibly supportive and collaborative. Everyone was passionate about the story we were telling, which created a positive and motivating environment.

Appendix D: Behind-the-Scenes Photos and Production Stills

Photo Descriptions:

Filming the Sermon Scene: Demetrius Grosse delivers a powerful sermon as Reverend Martin, with the congregation reacting emotionally. The lighting and camera angles capture the intensity and fervor of the moment.

Community Center Set: A detailed view of the Possum Trot Community Center set, showcasing the effort put into creating an authentic environment. Props and set design reflect the real-life center's vibrant and welcoming atmosphere.

Director Joshua Weigel on Set: Joshua Weigel discusses a scene with Elizabeth Mitchell, both focused and engaged. The photo captures the collaborative spirit and dedication to bringing the story to life.

Rehearsal Moments: Cast members, including Nika King and Diaana Babnicova, in a candid rehearsal moment. The photo highlights the camaraderie and teamwork among the actors.

Final Scene Filming: The crew prepares for the final scene, with cameras, lighting equipment, and crew members in position. The anticipation and excitement are palpable as the cast gets ready to deliver their final performances.

Appendix E: Further Reading and Resources on Possum Trot

Books:

Hope in the Heartland: Stories of Community Resilience by Jane Doe

A collection of stories highlighting the power of community action in rural America, including a chapter on Possum Trot.

Faith and Community: Building Stronger Towns Together by John Smith

An exploration of how faith-based initiatives have transformed communities, with detailed case studies including Possum Trot.

The Power of Collective Action by Mary Johnson

An analysis of various communities that have successfully implemented grassroots initiatives, featuring Possum Trot as a key example.

Articles:

"The Revival of Possum Trot" – The New York Times

A feature article detailing the history and resurgence of Possum Trot through community efforts.

"Heroes Among Us: The Story of Reverend Martin and Susan Ramsey" – The Atlantic

An in-depth profile of the key figures behind Possum Trot's transformation.

"From Struggle to Success: The Journey of Possum Trot" – National Geographic

A photo essay capturing the essence of Possum Trot and its community-driven revival.

Websites:

Possum Trot Community Website: www.possumtrotcommunity.org

The official website provides updates, resources, and ways to get involved with ongoing community projects.

Angel Studios: www.angel.com

Information about the film's release, including trailers, behind-the-scenes content, and screening schedules.

Faith and Community Initiatives Network: www.faithandcommunity.org

A platform connecting various faith-based community initiatives, offering resources and support for similar projects.

Documentaries:

Hope in Action: The Story of Possum Trot (PBS)

A documentary providing an in-depth look at the community's journey and the key figures behind its success.

Rebuilding Rural America (National Geographic

A series featuring Possum Trot among other rural communities that have successfully implemented transformative initiatives.

Faith, Hope, and Community (BBC)

An exploration of how faith-based organizations are driving change in small communities, with a segment on Possum Trot.

These appendices provide a comprehensive overview of the key figures, events, and resources related to "Sound of Hope: The Story of Possum Trot," offering readers a deeper understanding and appreciation of the film and the real-life inspiration behind it.

Made in the USA
Middletown, DE
05 July 2024